AF423782

Soul of the Wild

The Wisdom of Elephants

Soul *of the* Wild

The Wisdom of Elephants

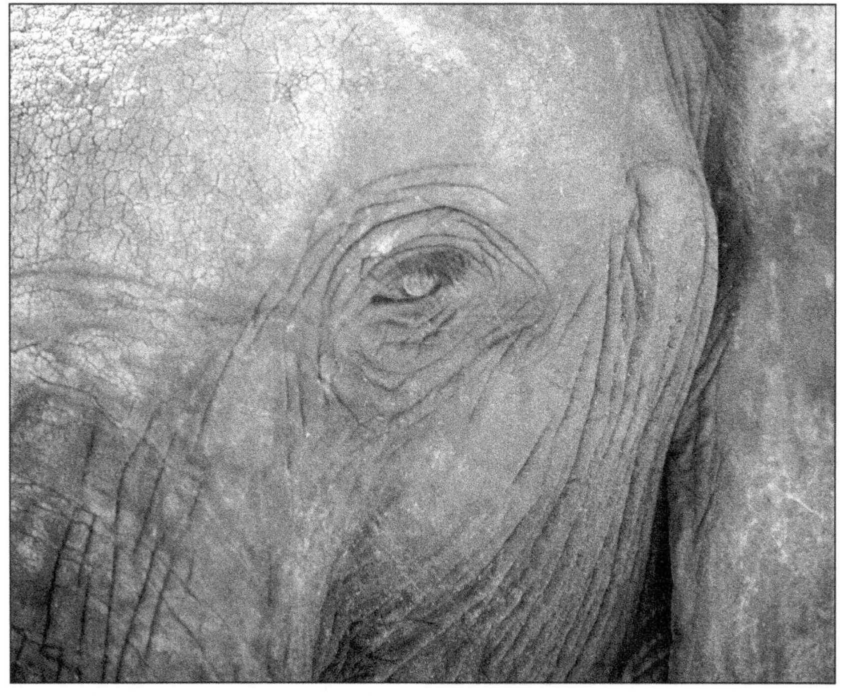

BOOK II

Barbara Shor, DVM

Soul of the Wild Publications
2023

CONTENTS

DISCLAIMER

Although I am trained as a wildlife veterinarian, this book does not come from that kind of mentality. Instead, it is a work from my heart and soul in connection and communion with that of the Elephants.

Some of the information that has come through my conversations with the group consciousness of elephants, or group soul, may not completely align with what scientists have learned or have come to believe about elephants. So please take what is written here with discernment, tapping into your own intuition as a "fact check." Sometimes our perceptions—or the elephants' perceptions—might differ from what others believe or perceive as true. Listen to your own inner knowing if you have any questions or concerns. If it feels true, wonderful. If not, just let it go.

Pronouns are difficult. I use "he" or "she" to describe individual animals, and "they" for more than one. The word "it" has its own connotations, and when used with an animal, it may be seen as meaning that animal doesn't have its own individual nature and personality. So I prefer to use "she" in some cases, and "he" in others, when describing individual animals.

Some names are capitalized at times, such as Elephants, Earth, Humanity. This denotes that there is a sacred aspect to this being or group of beings. I see them as Souls rather than simply physical beings or structures.

This book contains my conversations with the group consciousness, or collective consciousness, of animals rather than with individual animals. This form of communication is described in more detail in the book, in Chapter 2: *How Telepathic Communication Works*. We are speaking at the level of the soul, or higher aspect, of these animals, rather than with physical, tangible elephants.

I have been so honored and blessed to work with these astoundingly magnificent beings. I hope the words, thoughts, and ideas shared here will touch you as deeply as they have touched me.

A Note About the Typography

Four typefaces are used in this book to express my
points of view and the words of the Elephants:

This typeface represents my voice in the present time
and the general narrative of the book.

*This italics typeface is used to express my
inner thoughts and recollections of past events.*

**A stronger typeface expresses my questions and
comments when I'm in dialogue with the Elephants.**

And this elegant and distinctive typeface represents
the words of the Elephants in dialogue with me

ACKNOWLEDGEMENTS

This book has been an evolutionary journey. I was naive about the inner workings of animals, believing, as many do, that they are "just animals." I always loved and wanted to help animals, but wasn't sure how. I studied animal behavior: an observer. From there I became a veterinarian: a healer. And eventually, after a long road, now I am an animal communicator: a lover and spokesperson.

All along the way, the animals have been with me as teachers and guides. For this, I am eternally grateful. There have been many human teachers as well, all of whom have contributed greatly to my path. I am thankful for all of them. I have had many wise, compassionate mentors along the way. Thank you.

The support I received for *Soul of the Wild, the Wisdom of Elephants, Book II*, began with a writing group led by a fabulous editor, writer, and teacher, Shoshana Alexander. I learned a tremendous amount about writing from her over those five years, especially about expressing my heart and allowing myself to be vulnerable. I am grateful to Shoshana for these teachings. The group became truly honest and open with one another and we all became better writers. Those writers, Bill Kastenberg, Judy Hilyard, and Carolyn Shaffer, enriched my life as a person and an author. Thank you all.

A big thank you to Avantika Mathur, with whom I am producing *Animals and Us: Voices of a New Paradigm*, a podcast focused on animal communication and consciousness. We interview amazing guests doing fabulous work. Avantika has been supportive of my work and what we create together as co-hosts and friends is joyful and inspiring for me!

Wonderful friends have supported me. I have been in a "heart circle" and a "dream group" with lovely women who helped me become who I am today. Thank you all.

I especially want to thank Ginna and David Gordon of Lucky Valley Press, my editors/publishers. They are both conscious, loving souls who really get what this work is about. Ginna supported and encouraged me in our weekly conversations as I wrote *Soul of the Wild: The Wisdom of Elephants* and she helped me refine many things. David created a beautiful interior. I am deeply grateful for his excellent typography and design.

My sincere thanks to Chris Molé of Book Savvy Studio who designed the beautiful cover for this book. She is extremely creative and it was a pleasure to work with her.

And the Elephants; my dearly beloved teachers, guides, healers, mentors, and friends. It is hard to imagine that these gigantic other-worldly beings could actually be so wise, compassionate, and aware. But they are, beyond my previously wildest imagination. After we wrote the first book together, they didn't leave. In fact, they wouldn't leave me alone! It was the Elephants who encouraged me to write this second edition of *Soul of the Wild.* They had more to say.

It has been a magical process, working with these great beings. They have truly been my spiritual teachers and I am grateful and in awe. Thank you, blessed Elephants, for opening my heart and soul to ever expanding realities and perceptions. You have changed my life for the better, and I am profoundly grateful and honored to present your wise teachings to the world of Humankind.

FOREWORD

by Avantika Mathur

There come moments in our lives when we seek deeper meaning and purpose in our existence. We might want to know why things are the way they are, who we are really meant to be, and why we're here. A few years ago, I sent out a message to the cosmos – an announcement and a request. I wanted to understand myself as a spiritual being, and was eager to learn about the bigger picture, spiritually, of the world I lived in. What was the meaning of it all? What was I missing?

I wrote it in my journal and said it out loud in total surrender: "Show me, Universe. I'm here and I'm ready to learn. Tell me what I need to know."

One year later, when I found myself lost in the pages of *Soul of the Wild: Intimate Messages from the Elephants and Whales,* I knew in my heart that my journey to find answers had begun. I had been guided to this book.

It seemed that the elephants and the whales knew exactly who I was. As a matter of fact, they knew who we all are, as human beings, at our very core. They explained so eloquently what makes us unique and important, and why we struggle with things the way we do. They had a profound awareness about who they were too, as elephants and whales, with their special gifts and specific purposes on this planet. In great detail, and with love and compassion, they shared their perspectives on how we are all interconnected and how we all depend on each other, physically and energetically. They were wise, their perspectives were touching, and their messages were thought provoking.

Everything they shared made sense to me and felt deeply grounded in the truth. And as I made my way through the last few pages of the book, I felt emotional and humbled. I realized that the animals were going to be my greatest spiritual teachers.

What a beautiful gift Barbara had shared with me and with the world through this book. Her curious and heartfelt dialogue with these majestic beings was such a treat to read. It was like sitting down for a cup of coffee with a long-lost friend and exploring the world together through each other's eyes. It was magical and moving, and I learned more about elephants and whales than I ever could have through most books or documentaries. I had the opportunity and the privilege to get to know them on a soul level. Lucky me.

I knew I needed to meet Barbara and thank her for being able to do what she does, and for sharing her heart-to-heart conversations with the animals. When we finally met, I knew I had found a kindred spirit. While our differences in age, ethnicity, location, background, and upbringing made our life experiences so unique, we connected deeply in our appreciation and reverence for animals and the natural world. We talked for hours and hours about their spiritual lives, and how limited the world's perspectives were on who they really are. What would it be like if everyone understood how profound and wise animals are? What would happen if people saw communicating with animals telepathically as being natural, normal, and simply a part of who we are? How would that transform the way we treat each other and every living being?

Soon into our friendship, we realized how much we wanted to invite others into our conversations and build community. We wanted to bring together like-minded people who saw animals the way we did – as sacred, sentient, conscious, spiritual beings who we can learn from and evolve with. Together, Barbara and I launched our podcast, *Animals & Us – Voices of A New Paradigm.* It gave us a place to be our authentic selves, embrace our lived experiences, question society's worldviews, give voice to the animals who could then share their perspectives, interview fascinating people, and collectively dream of a world that is healing and transforming for the better.

Barbara and I also traveled to Botswana together. We experienced the beautiful Okavango Delta as we journeyed through the bush of Kasane, Chobe, Savuti, Khwai, and Moremi. Disconnected from technology and far from distractions, we had the opportunity to witness African wildlife in all its glory. We saw lions, cheetahs, leopards, giraffes, zebras, wildebeest, and baboons, just to name a few. Perhaps the most heartwarming and touching moments were those we experienced with the elephants. Being in their presence was deeply emotional and all encompassing. I felt "at home" with them, as if they knew me and recognized me for who I truly am when all superficial layers are stripped away.

On one occasion, while we were watching an elephant drink water from a pond, Barbara and I both received a message loud and clear from the elephant: "Take care of the Earth."

It was a simple but very important message to us humans. While we may not see these animals and interact with them in our daily lives, hundreds and thousands of miles away from them, it is we who must protect and guard our planet so that they can survive and thrive. The elephants, and all other beings, depend on us to do this, and to do it well.

Unfortunately, given what is happening in our world today, with issues like environmental degradation and loss of biodiversity, this reality seems far, far away. The human-nature divide is strong, and most people are too distracted and disconnected to recognize the true capacity of animals, and of ourselves.

In her second edition, *Soul of the Wild: The Wisdom of Elephants,* Barbara continues as an intermediary who asks tough and vulnerable questions on our behalf and interprets the guidance that the elephant consciousness has to offer during these challenging times. She asks them how they perceive challenges like climate change, global warming, and human population growth. She asks them to share practical insights and advice that we can implement as we navigate through the confusion, guilt, and grief that many of us are feeling. What the elephants share, as you will see, shows us how to focus on the light and love that is already within us. They remind us that the change must start from each one of us, and that we must commit to reconnecting with our higher nature and divine spark that already knows how to protect Earth and all her beings. These teachings have been instrumental in my own personal and spiritual journey, and I am forever grateful for them. They helped me discover who I am as a spiritual being and showed me that all the answers I need are already within me.

The natural world is waiting patiently for each of us - to awaken, to remember, and to step into the next evolution of humanity that can "incorporate love, peace, and honor for all life." Thank you, Barbara, for bringing ancient elephant wisdom to us and helping us remember who we are and what we need to do.

INTRODUCTION

I have always loved elephants, but it took many years to know who they truly are. A big treat for me as a child was going to the circus with my Dad. My very favorite act was Gunther Gable Williams, supreme wild animal trainer, riding atop huge elephants around the circus ring. I thought he was amazing and I loved seeing those beautiful animals. Years later, after graduating from veterinary school, I went to Chicago to visit the veterinarian who worked for the Barnum and Bailey Circus. I had met him at an American Association of Zoo Veterinarians meeting, where he invited me to stay at his house in Chicago. This is where the circus was based. He said he would introduce me to Gunther. How could I possibly refuse?

And so, I got to meet the premier circus master, Gunther Gable Williams. I had expected to meet a tall, handsome, strong character, that animals served simply out of love and respect. Gunther was shorter than I had thought he might be, but every bit as charismatic. I was in awe!

I learned from my friend, the veterinarian, that Gunther arrived at the circus very early every day, long before sunrise, to greet all of his animals and give them some loving attention and care. I was still mightily impressed and felt extremely privileged to be in his presence.

* * *

Some years later, my fantasy bubble completely deflated. I learned how animals are treated in the circus. I have no idea at this point if Gunther was as cruel and demanding as some other trainers, but I am sure it was not a wonderful life for those animals: living in small cages, traveling nonstop, performing several times a day, doing what Gunther commanded them to do or else... I don't know what the animals suffered when they didn't perform to his standards, but I can only imagine it wasn't all that pleasant. So my gigantic infatuation with Gunther and love for the circus evaporated in a major way.

The other activity I loved as a child was going to the Cincinnati Zoo, not far from my home. I knew all the names of each species of animal. I had learned them from my father, who was passionate about wild animals and read about them in nature and wildlife magazines constantly, for as long as I can remember. I had no real thoughts about the plight of elephants in the zoo, who were living in cages, pacing back and forth out of boredom. To me, this was normal behavior and I just accepted it.

Years later, I volunteered at the Denver Zoo before attending Colorado State University College of Veterinary Medicine. I loved being around and working with those animals. During my final year of veterinary school, I did a three month internship at the Denver Zoo. I followed the veterinarian during his daily excursions in the zoo, recording all the events of the day. In the evening I wrote a daily log that was distributed to all zoo employees.

Once, when the vet was away, I was in charge. I had to give an injection of Penicillin to one of the elephants. It was a huge syringe and I was scared to death, but I did it. The keeper distracted her by making her lift one front leg while I injected her on the other side. She remained calm, but I was sure glad when it was over! That was as close as I ever got to a live elephant.

Pursuing my love of wildlife, after graduating from veterinary school I did a residency in non-domestic animal medicine at University of California, Davis, Veterinary School. Among other things, I served as veterinarian at the Sacramento and Micke Grove zoos in California.

Still, I had no idea about the inner workings of these animals. To me, zoos were places where elephants and other animals lived so that people could enjoy them and learn about them. I was so naive.

Yes, animals are there for our enjoyment and education. Sometimes even for captive breeding for species survival or to aid with wildlife conservation. Some people, like me, have our first live contact with these animals in zoos or other captive environments and may go on to serve them in some way. And some zoos have come a long way, treating animals as well as possible in a captive environment.

But at what cost to the animals? It is something I have thought about and struggled with for many years now. Do conscious, sentient, compassionate, wise beings deserve to live in cages, no matter how large or seemingly "suitable" or "humane?" Is putting animals in solitary confinement or with very limited range of motion truly humane? I don't think so.

I have had a tremendous change of heart since my younger years when I thought animals were "just animals." Now I know they are so much more.

I didn't even know how much I adored elephants until I lived in Kenya for a year, from 1989 to 1990. While there, I participated in a Cape Buffalo research project for a month in Masai Mara National Reserve. It was the most magical month of my life. I describe this experience in more detail later in the book, Chapter 4 *African Night.*

Each evening, before dinner, the elephants came to the meadow behind our tents. I can still hear the squeaky sound of grass being pulled out of the ground, wrapped delicately in their dexterous trunks and then deposited in their mouths. I delighted at their antics as the young bulls sparred together, clashing tusks against one another. And I loved watching babies suckling contentedly on their calm mothers.

The peace and joy I experienced in the presence of those elephants was something I will never forget. It was then that my true love for them started to expand and grow. And my life soon changed in dramatic ways.

Not long after my year in Africa, I left veterinary practice and dedicated much of my time to my emotional and spiritual growth. And I started speaking with animals telepathically, as a professional animal communicator. That became my life's work.

In 2002, I returned to Africa and stayed three months in Namibia, South Africa, and Kenya. I saw abundant wildlife and, to my delight, many elephants. But it wasn't until I got home that I realized the Elephants came with me. I could feel their presence energetically and it was strong enough that I had to pay attention. The full story is in the book, Chapter 1 *The Elephants' Call*. It was then that these conversations began and the original book was born.

* * *

This book is the story of my love affair with elephants. But, as a child, I wasn't aware of their inner life or my own. I was raised in a culture that saw animals as commodities rather than beings to be revered. It took years before I could acknowledge my own sensitive, intuitive, and empathic nature fully and see animals for who they are as spiritual beings. I am grateful that now I am able to communicate with Elephants telepathically and share their beautiful teachings with you.

AUTHOR'S NOTE

For months, I fought against rewriting my first and only book, *Soul of the Wild: Intimate Messages from the Hearts and Souls of Elephants and Whales.* I wanted to get on with it and write a brand-new book with current, exciting material. From all different species. But my inner guidance wouldn't leave me alone. Elephants and Whales, along with my own Soul and Divine guidance, continued to tell me that the information in my first book was important and needed to be presented in a new way, along with deeper, more advanced communications from the Elephants and Whales. And not only that, I was then guided to separate these newer versions into individual books for each species. So there would be a series of books, starting with Elephants, and then on to other species from there. Finally, I gave in.

Writing a book is not easy, and, for me, rewriting a book is even more challenging. It is not the new writing that is hard. That part comes easily and I love the process. When I can tune into the Elephants, the words simply flow through me with very little effort. It is the editing that is demanding and tedious for me. Wrote that, read that, and now I have to read it yet again? What is most difficult for me is to combine old writings and new material and figure out what goes where, what gets left out, and how to weave it all together.

One day I was working on this integration process when I just felt frustrated and tired of it all. So I asked a new question of the Elephants, just to change the atmosphere. But before they shared any new information, they spoke to me personally. Here is what they said:

* * *

We want to honor you for what you do. You always think it is not enough, but it truly is. The work we do together is universal, for a higher purpose than simply writing a book together. And this is what we want to explain.

Each time we connect there is an energy transfer. We see you and you see us. But more than that. We share one another's lives, and, in this way, we are able to create an understanding that transcends earthly reality for both humans and elephants. Said another way, when we connect in this way and share our hearts and our thoughts, we illuminate greater understanding, acceptance, love, and respect for all of us. It is this, dearest one, that will change the world. If all beings, including all people, could simply learn to love and respect one another, there would be no wars, violence, abuse, exploitation, or harm in any way. We would realize that we are all one consciousness, and to hurt one being means to hurt all. To love one means to love all.

We recognize that rewriting this book is a lot of effort and can be quite tedious. It is not always fun. But it is important, and each time you go through the words we have written together, it deepens the process of communication, communion, and understanding.

Thank you again for loving us and for doing this work. We are truly all in it together. And it is books like this, work like this, love like this, that will heal a deeply disgruntled world.

This was so helpful. I realized that my small ideas about working with these great creatures had been so limited and self-centered. Now I saw that the loving, blessed connection I have with them, reinforced by this writing, is what is most important. And it can have an impact on so many others.

And so, my dearest, beloved readers, my hope and prayer for you is that, through reading this book, you too will create your own warm and loving connection with the Elephants. You then will be a conduit for healing, for yourself as well as for Elephants and all living beings.

We, as little human selves, have no idea of the consequences of our actions on a bigger scale. The love we share goes well beyond our perceived narrow sphere of influence. Perhaps, by the simple act of loving, we will save the world as we now know it, for ourselves and future generations.

ELEPHANT GREETINGS

Welcome, dear friends! Thank you for joining us.

This book is our attempt to introduce you to our world. As Elephants embodied on Earth, we'd love to share with you our perspectives and perceptions. We come in bodies that may seem strange to you, very different from your own. And yet we share a common interior world which is, at this point, still remote, misunderstood, and underestimated by most people.

Yes, there are many who study elephants and are well versed in our attitudes, behaviors, and culture. But that is not really what this book is about. You can find that information in numerous other sources. This book is our attempt to inform you about who we are at the deepest level. As souls. As fellow inhabitants of this great planet. Our beloved Mother Earth does her best to hold us all in her loving embrace as we evolve together as Souls.

We do not pretend to present the Truth. In fact, as we see it, there is not one ultimate truth. There are many interpretations of what can be perceived as true. But we bring you our perspective, and that is all we can do. It is up to you to trust your own discernment and intuition to know what holds true for you. All we can do is present our point of view.

May this book be an opening for you, an invitation to find your own way. If you can hold in your heart a strong and clear intention for peace on Earth, for well-being for all her inhabitants, for love to reign in all dimensions, and for human beings to evolve at a rapid pace in order to preserve what has been given to all of us, we can all make it through these challenging times on our beloved home.

Earth is not an easy planet. We all have challenges, as well as moments of joy and delight. Our wish for you is that you will feel just a little lighter and, at the same time, more in touch with your own capacity to love, to understand, and to have compassion for others by reading this book.

We do not claim to be perfect. No one is. But because of our experiences on Earth, combined with the wisdom passed down through generations, as well as a transcendent connection with deeper realms of existence, we feel we have a great deal to share. And now is the time.

We sense profound changes happening on Earth. There is rampant fear, anger, and sadness in the human world. We see it, feel it, and know it. And we want to help. We know that chaos precedes transformation and we want to show you that all is not lost. Many of us are working toward peace and harmony for all life on Earth. You are truly not alone. And hope is a great healer. This is what we offer you now, as you tread through difficult circumstances.

As you read this book, we are with you, loving you and enveloping you in peace. The words are only guides to get you to the greater consciousness that is our home base. You may feel it. You may dream it. You may embody it. No matter how you receive the messages contained in these writings, please know that we love and support you in your own personal transformation, as well as that of our beautiful Mother Earth and all her creatures.

Once you know, beyond all doubt, that we, as Animal Souls, have wisdom to share, perhaps you can look a bit differently at all other beings who live on this great Earth. Life is abundant here. Hopefully it always will be. We trust that through our words, thoughts, feelings, ideas, and suggestions, you might discover an entirely new world about you and within you.

We love you, dear human beings. Because you show interest in this book, we know that you are open-minded and open-hearted. Our greatest desire is for you to become the next evolution of humanity that can incorporate love, peace, and honor for all life. And we know you can.

Thank you so much for joining us on this great adventure called Life. We invite you to explore further into your own inner depths to find ways to connect more deeply with yourself, with all creatures, with the natural world, and with our dear Mother Earth.

Thank you, thank you, thank you, and we wish for you lives of great love, deep joy, and miraculous adventures.

CHAPTER 1

THE ELEPHANTS' CALL

It is a splendid day in Namibia, an arid country located on the southwestern border of Africa. I am visiting my friend, Betsy, also an American veterinarian. Betsy and I met 13 years ago in Kenya and while I left to go back to the U.S., she landed a job in Namibia. Since that time she has worked as a wildlife research ranger, specializing in elephants and rhinos, for the Namibia Ministry of Environment and Tourism.

We have driven through the desert all day to get to the base camp for a rhino census; now we are camped in a remote oasis with all kinds of interesting characters. There are camel herders with their camels, an array of native rhino trackers, and some rugged white men, reminiscent of the old African big game hunters. There are also cooks and other laborers who live in tents in this temporary little outpost.

The next day, Betsy and I spend the day riding in an open truck with native trackers, searching for rhinos. It is a thrilling experience to be in this wild, open desert, living with indigenous people, most of whom do not speak English. Our trackers are incredibly good at interpreting signs of rhinos and other creatures. Even so, we find plenty of rhino dung and tracks, but no rhinos.

We do, however, see elephants. They are feeding in a green treed meadow next to our campsite by a beautiful little streambed. Betsy and I sit quietly and watch this small herd as they eat. Gentle creatures, quiet and peaceful, they move about slowly, paying us little mind. I experience a feeling of utter well-being and quietude here, in the presence of these magnificent animals. No words. No thoughts. Just peace. And deep love for the elephants. I am very grateful to be here.

A couple days later, Betsy and I drive her truck to Etosha National Park, the premier wildlife park of Namibia, to spend a few days. Much of the ground in this park is chalky white, comprised of dried up salt pans. The name "Etosha" means "place of dry water."

One beautiful, sunny afternoon, Betsy and I are out for a drive through the park. We have seen lots of animals, including giraffes, gemsbok, springbok, zebras, and an assortment of birds, and we are now on our way back to the lodge for the night. They close the gates at sunset and if you are not back inside the compound by closing, you are out of luck. Sleeping in the truck does not seem an inviting possibility, so we need to get back soon.

We see a group of elephants along the roadside not far from the lodge. Despite our concern for the time, we stop and watch the mothers and babies walk past us, seemingly not paying any attention to us. The babies are utterly adorable, walking next to their huge mothers and sometimes running, little trunks flailing, to catch up with them.

It is getting late and the sun is almost down, so we drive on. As we round a curve in the road, Betsy suddenly slams on the brake. In the middle of the road stands a behemoth: a gigantic bull elephant, facing us head on. For a moment my heart stops. The elephant is obviously startled too. He shifts back and forth from one front foot to the other, ears outstretched, trunk raised, looking directly at us. He is clearly disturbed and deciding what to do.

The realization hits Betsy and me that this guy could destroy our little truck, and both of us, without any effort at all. We are completely at his mercy.

When we catch our breath, we simultaneously feel the urge to send love to this elephant. All the years of loving elephants and being in their presence, physically and spiritually, come back to me and I feel my deep, abiding love for them that has always been present. This bull is not just a big creature standing in the road, but a beloved friend, a fellow soul, and I relate to him on this level. Betsy, who has worked with elephants for years, does the same. We let him know telepathically, through our loving connection, that we will not harm him and that we need to get on our way.

Immediately, he seems to relax. The shifting stops, his ears come down, and his trunk lowers and softens. He watches us for a few moments, then moves to the side of the road, as if nothing has happened, and walks on.

For a few moments, Betsy and I sit stunned and silent in the truck. Something happened that we can't make sense of in this dazed state—a meeting of minds, a communion of souls—beyond what we understand rationally. And I sense that this is an important moment.

I had no idea at the time, but this magnificent bull elephant, crashing so abruptly into my life, was a messenger, a harbinger of things to come. He relayed a subtle yet powerful communication from the consciousness of all elephants that embedded itself in my own consciousness.

Within two months, I was back in the United States, feeling the unseen, energetic presence of elephants with me. For several years I had been communicating telepathically with animals, both domestic and wild, including elephants. So I knew what it felt like to sense the presence of animals with me and to feel "summoned" by them.

Thus, when I began hearing the elephants speaking to me, I paid attention.

What I heard was that they wanted to write a book with me. They wanted people to know who they really are at the deepest level, and they wanted me to be their spokesperson.

I had already written much of what I thought would be my first book called *Soul of the Wild*, comprised of conversations I'd had with numerous animal species. So when the elephants asked me to write a book, I was surprised and quite resistant at first. I already had a book! But they persisted and let me know that the information would be deeper than what I had received before. So finally, I agreed.

And that is how this book began. For months after that, I sat at my computer every morning and "took dictation." The experiences were deeply impactful for me.

Shortly after the elephants and I began writing together, I experienced what seemed to be an initiation into their world.

I feel pressure in my head and my breathing is rapid and shallow as I begin to hyperventilate. I can feel my head getting tighter and tighter, and more painful. And now that tension is starting to focus in my temples.

Suddenly, in my mind's eye, I see the temporal glands of a female elephant, located just where the tension is in my head, and I see dark fluid staining the sides of her face. I know these glands secrete fluid when there is strong emotion. I can actually feel those glands on my own face. It is as if I am merged with the elephant and feeling her feelings, emotionally and physically.

Now I feel cold air rushing from my chest into my throat. It feels like the icy cold of winter breath. A thought enters my mind: "The ice is melting."

I breathe through this, feeling the cold in my throat and the tension in my head, crying all the while. Finally, I begin to relax.

I hear a message that seems to come directly from the Elephants. They say that in the past, when I communicated with animals, I feared being swept away by their pain and so I separated myself from them; hence, the ice around my heart.

Now, after some self-healing, I can be with the animals in their pain as well as their joy, and I can handle it without losing myself. Therefore, I can communicate with them at a more profound level.

After this, I sat down at my desk every morning and allowed the Elephants to be with me, through my writing. Sometimes I asked questions, other times I simply asked what they wanted to share. I was often astounded by their wisdom.

Sometimes their information stretched me to my limits and I asked over and over again if it was really true. Or I requested clarification. I was so moved at times, I wept as I wrote and could not speak for hours, touched by a feeling of profound connection. Always, always, I felt their unconditional love and deep wisdom. They became my primary teachers; I opened to new insights, concepts, and ways of viewing the world.

The following chapters are messages I received directly from the consciousness of Elephants. I have organized them according to topics for easier understanding, but the conversations simply flowed from day to day according to my moods and questions, and what the elephants chose to share.

The Elephants say that the messages—the words and concepts— are not the most important part of this writing. They are vehicles to pave the way for something greater. The true purpose of this book is to allow the energy and consciousness of Elephants to flow through the written pages so that readers may physically, emotion- ally, and spiritually experience the profound connection I have felt with these majestic animals while receiving their transmissions. The book is a beginning, an opening to the wild and wondrous world of Elephants, as well as a doorway for exploring your own connection with all living beings.

CHAPTER 2

HOW TELEPATHIC COMMUNICATION WORKS

My dear Elephant friends, can you tell me more about your methods of communication?

There are two areas of our communication that captivate people. One is the actual vocalizations, which include our infrasonic sounds. The other is telepathic. Some people think of us as intelligent, sensitive, emotional beings. We are that, but what we refer to in this book goes beyond this. And, as you know, it applies to more than only elephants. The language we share with you here is different from the sounds humans study. The scientific community is excited about the latter and extremely skeptical about the former. This is as it should be.

Why?

Because if the scientific community were open-minded about all possibilities, the scientific process, as it is now, might run amok. There would be no structure. Your culture is based on structure. This process needs to proceed slowly. It is easy for people to understand what they can measure, as they do with our vocalizations. It is something concrete to which they can relate.

However, the language of telepathic communication is not measurable and is another story. It challenges everything most people believe is true or even possible. Denying the reality of this type of communication keeps people stuck in a paradigm that easily dishonors others.

What if, all of a sudden, everyone on the planet knew that animals think, feel, and speak? What would happen to your infrastructure? It would fall apart. Why? Because people would know that it is absolutely inhumane to treat animals as they are treated today.

But people know that other people have feelings, and still there is abuse amongst humans.

You are right. It doesn't stop people from abusing other people. Obviously, other humans can think, feel, and speak, but there is still violence and abuse in the world. So why would it matter if people knew that animals are the same?

Here is why: in the beginning of human history, there was communication on all levels, without words. Things were direct, straight forward, and simple. This has changed dramatically. Over time it became necessary to have more detailed and specific communication as life gradually became more complex, and so language developed. Now there are many languages, each with its own nuances and interpretations according to the culture in which it is spoken. But basically, all verbal human language is similar in its essence.

With the advent of this complex system of language came a concurrent dwindling of the awareness of other forms of communication. Body language is not often part of everyday consciousness, especially with the introduction of telephones and computers. Telepathic communication has become obsolete, therefore misunderstood and even discounted.

We are living in a time in which this form of communication has been mostly unrecognized except by a few. That is changing. People are realizing that verbal communication, which encompasses written language, is not enough. The missing element is the spiritual component of language and communication.

Yes, words can powerfully evoke feelings and concepts. What is even more powerful is to evoke feelings and concepts without words. In this way, you go directly to the source of the thought or feeling.

What you do as a writer is to take concepts, ideas, thoughts, and feelings, and turn them into language so people can understand what you are trying to say.

Someday this will not be necessary. People will be so familiar with this telepathic way of being that they will not need interpreters. Now they do.

We do not demean or belittle what you do. You are far more than a translator. However, this element of what you do with us is important. Why? Because it opens people to their own gifts and their connection with the universe, with higher consciousness, with healing, and with their own inner guidance.

I understand. But what about the original question: why would people stop mistreating animals if they knew that we are all the same, in terms of consciousness? What difference would it make?

Yes, the question. Sometimes we get distracted. We cannot guarantee that humans would stop harming animals if they knew we are all the same. But what we are trying to get across to you, dear friend, is that if people actually knew, felt, and experienced for themselves that animals are simply another life form, not lesser than or all that different from humans, this might evoke a higher conscious awareness of the connectedness of all beings. And when you truly sense this connectedness, you enter spiritual realms where there is no violence or domination.

The awareness of unity inherently brings about love for self and others. Abuse and exploitation are not part of this reality. This is what we hope to evoke in those willing to go with us to this level of awareness.

Thanks for clarifying. I cannot imagine anything better than a world where all beings lived with love, honor, respect, reverence, and appreciation for one another.

TELEPATHIC COMMUNICATION

From your perspective, how does telepathic communication actually work?

Let's start with a premise: there are forces beyond those which human beings can perceive with their five senses. Not everything can be sensed physically or understood mentally.

Along with this premise is another: that we are all comprised of energy. It is all pervasive, not limited to physical bodies. It is contained within all things, or we may say, they are contained within it. Energy is everywhere and in everything.

Energy is not only on planet Earth. It is in the air and in planets and stars as well. In fact, it is what animates everything in the cosmos.

When you, as a person, meet with someone else, there is an energetic connection between you. This can manifest as an emotion, like love, disdain, fear, or trust. Sometimes you sense things without knowing the person and without knowing why. It comes from a different place than your earth-based senses. So what is it you are feeling in these cases? Some may call it intuition. But where does intuition come from?

From our perspective, intuition comes from a sense of knowing that transcends earthly reality, from energy that is beyond conscious awareness. In this sense, it is invisible and perhaps not aligned with what you might consider "rational" thought.

In the same way, there is a part of us—humans and animals alike— that exists beyond conscious, physical awareness. This we call the Soul. It is that part of someone that exists energetically but not physically. And because it exists in this energy environment, what some call Spirit, it can operate beyond physical laws.

In this realm of Spirit, there is no time or space as it is perceived on Earth. A Soul can move about without the restrictions of an earthly body. It exists in a state of freedom, not limited by physical constraints. It can also communicate without impediments, simply through thought and intention. This is what is called telepathic communication.

In some cultures, people learned to communicate in this way. It was natural for them and they used it all their lives. This is still true with some indigenous peoples. But it was far more widely accepted years ago. Now, in many societies, telepathic communication is perceived as unreal, and by some, even harmful.

Some people are naturally born with this skill. Others learn it later in life.

I was someone who learned it later in my life. I think I was always empathic with animals, and probably telepathic as well. But I didn't realize it until after I had graduated from veterinary school.

I was immersed and educated in a culture that believed that only "real" things can be sensed with the five senses and their existence can be proven. In science and medicine, even still, as far as I can tell, double blind studies are the standard of proof. But telepathic communication is subtle and is sensed energetically, not physically. And mostly it cannot be proven using conventional means.

What I now realize is that had I allowed myself to be as empathic as I now am, there is no way I could have survived the things I needed to do in order to have all the experiences I have had with animals. I never could have made it through veterinary school, a veterinary residency, working in zoos and research labs, or being in the field doing wildlife research. Had I known then what I know now, I wouldn't have been able to bear the way animals are often treated by human beings. So, in its own way, my ignorance was what granted me the privilege of a life spent with a wide variety animals in a host of different environments.

Why did I need to do these things after all? Why not just stop?

As I understand it now, it was necessary for me to have these experiences and all the knowledge gained from them. They have given me a much deeper understanding of and compassion for a wide variety of animals. They have also given me credibility as I have stepped outside the mainstream, speaking on behalf of animals.

Yes, we see that. Sometimes we need to do things we may not understand at the time, but are guided to by our souls and higher motivations. It is important to follow those callings.

Back to telepathic communication. It is a practice that needs to be developed, and may take time.

Yes, each person differs in the way they communicate, depending on which abilities are stronger. Some are able to hear (clairaudient), others see (clairvoyant), others feel emotions or physical sensations (clairsentient), certain people smell odors that don't have a physical source (clairalience), and some just know things (claircognizant) without necessarily knowing how. And, these are often combined.

There are some who perceive the sensations of animals or other beings in their own bodies. Others communicate through symbols, images, or metaphors. And to some, the messages come through their waking or sleeping dreams.

It seems that communication in this way, between beings, is not only possible but a natural part of life. It may occur in ways people are not aware of, but they seem to know things they could not otherwise know. It may then be called intuition, synchronicity, coincidence, or a good guess. But when that person explores what is happening at a deep level, they may see that they communicate telepathically without their conscious knowledge.

Animals communicate telepathically with one another all the time. We have not taken on human constructs that say this doesn't exist. It is part of our nature; we accept it as such. Humans have lost this ability out of a need to conform to human-created rules that deny the existence of that which can't be experienced with the physical senses and awareness. But open and willing people can be taught to override these conditioned beliefs and then communicate telepathically with other beings. It is a matter of intent and focus.

*****

What about the work I do, called Animal or Interspecies Communication, with you and others? What really happens?

When we communicate with you, far more than words are relayed. We transmit thoughts and feelings, attitudes and perceptions that words cannot describe. Words are important, concepts and ideas are interesting; but what really occurs, and what is most impactful, is beyond the mind's comprehension. The mind wants to know what the heart and soul already know.

We are extremely emotional beings, and so, in large part, we live in the realm of the heart. These transmissions, however, go even beyond this realm. As we relay messages to you, we are opening up a new vortex of energy that connects all beings. The words are a vehicle to relay information, and behind the words is an energy of love and deep communion that cannot be expressed through language.

To explain this further, when you open up your energy field to communicate with us on this level (and we want to emphasize *this* level, meaning the one from which this book is written), you experience a loss of individual ego-based identity in order to merge with us energetically. This is why you may see your work as a cone, beginning with you as the base point and extending upward and outward, as the cone widens.

This cone expands into greater and greater realities until finally it reaches the level of All That Is, or universal consciousness. You can then connect with any part of consciousness: from other individuals to small or large groups of beings. It is up to you, as to where you focus your attention.

For instance, you can speak with one of us, or to the group of bulls or matriarchs, or the group of circus animals or zoo animals, or African or Asian elephants, or the consciousness of Elephants as a whole. And you can even go beyond this to call in the consciousness of all animals. There is no limit because energy is infinite, and at this level of communication, you can reach and relate to whomever and whatever you choose.

Thank you for this explanation. It helps me better understand what I do, especially when I communicate with an entire species, as I do here with you, dear Elephants.

Love is the driving force that allows this to take place. Love is an energy of expansion and acceptance, of allowing all possibilities. However, the energy we speak of goes even beyond what most people think of as love.

In the universal sense, love encompasses all. However, in your human reality, you carry notions about love that have been handed down over centuries and may limit your perspective about genuine love. Love itself is not limited. It is your ideas about love that limit your perception of what is possible and what occurs.

When we communicate with you, as we do now, we bypass these limiting ideas. We simply come into your being, as you allow us to, and relay our sense of what is. You receive it as you are able. Sometimes you are tired or sad, so you are not able to receive as much. At other times, you are wide open.

The messages we deliver here are universal; the concepts and ideas, the heart opening, the mind expansion, the connection with universal consciousness, is not limited to one race, species, or country. What we say here applies to all people everywhere, as well as to all animals and beings on this planet. We call it universal rather than simply global because the principles are universal. The applications are global.

I appreciate what you have been saying and I do have another question. I know that you do not speak in words to me. Can you explain how this works, so I can write down in words what you relay to me?

When we interact with you, we are projecting our thoughts, feelings, and ways of being to you and through you. Because you are so deeply connected with us energetically, you receive what we transmit immediately and effortlessly. You feel it in your entire being; you sense our emotions, understand our reality, grasp concepts, and align with us in all ways.

Because, as human, you interact with others through language, verbal and written, your wonderful brain immediately, automatically, reframes the concepts and sensations into words. Sometimes the words flow easily. Sometimes the concepts are difficult to understand at first so we clarify them. Your own conscious awareness will work with the ideas further until you can express them satisfactorily and appropriately. And sometimes, there are simply no words that accurately portray what you are receiving. At those times, we ask you to simply be with us and feel the energy pouring through you.

Is this enough? Or do you need something else? We sense there is something more.

This is one of those times when I can't even express what is going on. I feel there is more I need to know, but I don't even know what it is. Maybe you can help me with this and answer the question I am unable to ask.

Yes. We sense your question. It goes far beyond what your conscious mind can allow right now. So it is inaccessible to you, but we will attempt to answer anyway. For many years now you have questioned this process and how it works, and whether or not it is authentic. Your mind is strong and you know you have many internal voices. It has been a great challenge to decipher what is what. And since you do not usually see us, or hear us in a different voice from your own thoughts, you wonder if our voice is trustworthy and real.

Yes, and my insecurities come to the surface. You would think after all this time I would not question any longer. But I do.

And this is fine! It is what keeps you clearly authentic. If you did not question and just assumed everything you receive is true, you could easily be misled and follow the wrong path. So we are glad you question. Curiosity is a great thing, but too much doubt can be harmful. Sometimes you walk a fine line, but you are getting much clearer about this. So let us respond to your concern.

If you look at the world as it is today, you see greed and violence. Consensus reality asks you to buy into a world full of fear, greed, revenge, and many other negative emotions. Doubt and skepticism are a part of this reality. The idea of "love" has become romanticized to an unrealistic fantasy, often leading to frustration and anger. People simply cannot meet their own unrealistic expectations set in place by a culture with misguided values.

The love you feel for us and from us, particularly because we are not present with you physically, is seen by many as unreal, without any truth or value. Because you have been raised and conditioned in this context, you easily latch onto these ideas. However, we want to say that the love you feel here is as deep and real as anything anyone else can feel for anyone or anything. And because of this love, a gateway is open between our worlds.

Love allows you to be merged, or blended, with us energetically. It is what allows our messages to flow through you. And hopefully, this same love will allow and inspire others to commune with us as well.

We sense this is what you needed to know and now there is peace. We are glad you were willing to ask, yet again, even though your conscious mind did not want to go here. It is important to acknowledge your own feelings and do whatever is necessary in order to be at peace.

Thank you, beloved teachers. It seems you know me better than I know myself. What a great gift you are for me.

CHAPTER 3

THE ELEPHANTS' MISSION

Please describe your role and purpose on planet Earth.

We are an ancient force on this land. We came long ago in other forms: as mammoths, mastodons, and others. Now we are more refined. We have lived through changes in climate, geography, habitat, and in relationship to other species, including humans, but we have always retained the mission.

The function we serve on Earth, now as then, is to hold the vibration of the land intact and stable. We create an energy field around and within the Earth that grounds and balances the energy of the planet.

As we walk on the Earth, we radiate peace. We are highly emotional beings, but we embody deep spiritual peace. You may imagine that creatures who react emotionally are turbulent at their core. But this is not true. Each being has a persona that may be quite different from their soul essence. We can be aggressive and reactive here; but at our core, we are peace.

Our intent is to stabilize and harmonize the energy of planet Earth, bringing peace and well-being for all life forms, including the Earth herself. As we walk, our footsteps send out energy. This energy carries out our intent to create peace and stabilization. And, because we are large and our energy is even larger due to the dynamics of the group energy of our extended families, this effect carries far beyond our direct physical sphere of influence. It projects outward, like waves, to all points of the globe, stabilizing, harmonizing, and grounding energy everywhere.

We are containers for a certain type of energy, as are all species. Our form holds within it certain abilities, structures, and ways of being in the world that enable us to hold certain energetic principles, ideas, and manifestations. Each being is such a container. Form determines the role we play. But what we do is not limited by form. The form is a vehicle, or container, for expressing energetic patterns.

For instance, we are large and heavy-bodied. Because of this, our capacity to hold energy is considerable. As we move about, we have a powerful influence on large areas. The energy we hold and carry with us is intimately related to both our intent and purpose, which are intertwined. As we've said, it is our intent to bring peace to Earth, and to stabilize her energetically. We do this in several ways.

One way is simply through our presence, as carriers of this stabilizing energy. Another is through sounding. As we vocalize through sounds, including trumpeting, squealing, and rumbling, as well as infra-sounds[1], our energy is dispersed throughout the land and air and is sent to far-reaching places.

Our energy is also distributed through our footfalls. As we walk or run, our feet act as energy transmitters. They take our energy, filled

---

1   Infra-sounds are sounds of deep vibration, below the range of human hearing. In 1999, Dr. Katy Payne published her seminal book, *Silent Thunder*, which describes her discovery that elephants use infra-sounds to communicate over vast distances.

with our intent for stabilization and harmony, and impact the ground beneath our feet; this energy is pounded into the ground and dynamically carried into the air around us.

We are not the only creatures who have the capacity to transmit energy throughout the land, but because of our size, our ability to make sounds, and the way we are structured, we are able to energetically hold great areas intact and stable.

I had dinner once with a physicist friend. I told him about how your intent changes the energy of the planet through your sounds and movement. He said he was afraid for North America because there are few elephants here. He said that sound waves eventually dissipate, and he didn't understand how you can stabilize and harmonize the Earth's energy in distant locations.

Are there animals on this continent that serve the same function or do you truly impact distant places? Or, is it true that time and space are not an issue, even though this phenomenon seems to be partially a physical one in which molecules are actually changed?

As our energy impacts the Earth, the molecules are changed physically into a more refined vibration. But what is also true is that this is not solely a physical phenomenon. The physical and metaphysical operate together, not separately.

Molecules bombard one another and transfer information. At the same time, and in the same space, there is a non-physical action of energy transformation. There is no time or space in the spiritual realms, so the energy we impart to the environment is sufficient to transform the energy locally and non-locally.

What if it is true that all consciousness is linked? What if it is true that universal consciousness IS human consciousness, IS animal consciousness, IS plant and mineral consciousness, AND IS the consciousness of all that exists, living and non-living? And what if, through very clear intent, you are able to tap into this consciousness at will? In other words, you extend your capacity to feel, think, and know into all other dimensions and realities. In this way you are fully and totally connected with all beings and all that is.

From this place of connection (based on a mindset of openness and receptivity) all information, all of everything, is available to you, and IS you. This is who you truly are, at your core: a multidimensional being that is part of the great cosmic consciousness existing in all things, that IS all things.

It is from this place that you, or anyone else, can communicate with us telepathically. It is from this place that creation begins and that all can be known and all change can occur. Universal consciousness, or cosmic consciousness, is the power and energy that exists in everything, and when we speak about transforming energy, it is here that this exchange occurs.

To simplify: Let's say there is a female elephant named Bella. She lives in Africa with her biological family of offspring, aunts, and cousins. She is also part of a larger network of elephants, called a bond group in human language. As Bella and her family move throughout their range, and as they move in harmony with the larger bond group, and as the bond group moves in harmony with all elephants in this area and ultimately in all areas, there is an impact. The physical one is obvious. What is not so obvious to the human observer is the energetic impact and its implications.

One elephant can affect consciousness in a big way, just as one human being can. By simply being alive and holding a certain vibration and, because there is no time or space in Spirit, everything is influenced to some degree by that being's presence. Multiply this effect by the synchrony, the alchemy, that occurs when a group of souls comes together. Their influence is multiplied exponentially. A group of souls with a common intent is a powerful force in the universe. And so the influence of these beings is vast and enormous and not limited to one continent, since this dynamic operates in the spiritual planes as well as the physical.

For a moment, let us go back to the physical impact of molecules bombarding one another and affecting change. Is this like radio waves or the messages sent from satellites to television sets? Even though we can't see them, we know they are there because we hear and see the results.

This is simplistic, but it is a good model. And it is true that sound waves have limited range. However, suffice it to know that satellites and international radio waves do work, and that our way of influencing distant sites is not so different.

SOUND

Please tell me about your relationship to sound.

Sound is important for us. We use sound for many things—primarily to communicate with other elephants. But there is a higher purpose at work. We are not often aware of what we do. It is ingrained or "instinctive" in us. We use the word instinctive tentatively because it has certain connotations in your society. People often use this word to denote something inferior, as if the animal or person is doing something automatically and unconsciously, with no control, through instinct—as opposed to intellect, which is superior. We do not see it this way.

Instinct, as we see it, is a natural process that requires no conscious input. It is how nature operates and what sustains the Earth. We do not view it as inferior, but as the great operating principle that maintains and supports life.

Instinctively, we make sounds that resonate over vast distances. Each sound contains a certain vibration. As we sound, these vibrations travel through the air and the land. They carry a charge, a frequency. What happens is that the sound, as waves of energy, moves molecules of air or soil as it travels. It creates a kind of tunnel, or a breath of air, that moves other molecules in its path.

As these molecules of air or soil move, they take on a certain frequency, containing a pattern of energy. You can call this energy information, if you like, or memory, intelligence, or wisdom. These molecules begin to absorb the new frequency—information, memory, intelligence, wisdom—and transfer it to other molecules as they bump into one another.

The end result is that the entire frequency of an area changes. Because these sounds are of high intensity and carry the energy we impart to them—our own consciousness, our own vibration—these molecules are changed to resonate with our energy.

Because our highest intent is to hold a safe, sacred container for the Earth, to create a frequency of love and understanding, to impart ancient wisdom from our ancestors, and to help create a loving, peaceful network on this planet, that is the energy carried through our sounds. Therefore, it is the energy we impart to the Earth.

If we are abused, exploited, killed, or harmed in any way, we may become angry and withdrawn. You can imagine what that does to our energy and our sounds; they become distorted. The original energy of love and sharing is disrupted. And so the Earth suffers as well.

What are the implications of this?

Enormous. Because, as it is our mission to sustain the energy of the Earth as a loving, conscious, supportive being, our suffering contributes to the discord that occurs everywhere. Our energy is far-reaching. And so the whole Earth suffers as we do.

This is awful. I can see how this would contribute to violence in humans as well. It is a vicious cycle: violence begets violence. It seems hopeless. Humans have a long history of aggression and brutality and I do not see that this will change any time soon. I also don't see how human encroachment on elephant habitat will change. So is this planet doomed to the annihilation of all life as we know it? Is there any reason to hope things can change enough to prevent this from occurring?

You forget one thing: the power of prayer. We don't refer to prayer the way many people do. Prayer is a way of being. It is holding love and harmony in your heart and extending that to others. It is living in a state of higher consciousness, where everything and everyone are one loving energy, one vibrating, pulsing being that lives as one body with one heart.

It seems unlikely that this change could occur in your lifetime. War seems to predominate right now. Killing elephants and many other beings seems to be the pattern. This could go on indefinitely. Humanity seems to be heading in this direction. But there is a way out. Once people realize and know in the depths of their being that we are all one loving family, that we are all interconnected and related energetically, there will be peace on Earth. It cannot be otherwise.

CHAPTER 4

AFRICAN NIGHT

Living in East Africa in 1989–90 was the best year of my life. And the highlight was a month spent in Kenya's Masai Mara Game Reserve, the northern portion of Tanzania's Serengeti National Park.

I was involved with a Cape buffalo study, working with a Canadian wildlife veterinarian, Lars Karstad, and his wife, Martha, and a Kenyan veterinary technician, Tobias. As part of their training program, Kenyan veterinarians worked with us periodically. We always had a guard with us for protection.

Our mission: to dart buffalo with a tranquilizer gun to draw blood samples, in order to check titers to Rinderpest, a devastating disease that had killed many animals years before.

We drove through this lush, vibrant environment, searching for buffalo every day. I was awed by the numbers and variety of wild animals, from little mongooses scurrying through the grasses to magnificent tall giraffes eating the leaves of acacia trees. I especially loved watching lion prides as they relaxed and nuzzled one another during the day, before or after a great hunt. This was paradise.

In the evenings we sat by our tents, talking and reviewing the day. Our little cluster of tents sat in a huge green meadow of grasses dotted with Thompson's gazelles, zebras, wildebeest, and an infinite array of bird species. Surrounding this meadow was a curtain of greenery—large trees and bushes hiding the wilds beyond.

Every day, just before sunset, a herd of about 200 elephants came from behind the trees to graze in our meadow. Mothers and their calves ate together, silently. Occasionally two babies chased one another, playing with great gusto. Often young bulls sparred with their tusks. And adult bulls chased cows, often for a very long time until the cow finally submitted to this massive beast at least twice her size.

As these magnificent creatures moved slowly about, I loved to listen to the squeaky sound of grasses being pulled out of the earth by large trunks. "Elephant Lady" became my new name, fondly given to me by my companions because I adored these animals so much.

After dinner, on our last night in the Mara, the others go to their tents to sleep. I read by lantern light, sitting in front of my tent as I usually do, until my eyes get heavy and then I, too, retire to my cozy little cot, lulled to sleep by the laugh-like calls of hyenas and deep grunts of lions that seem to bore a hole right into my soul.

Just before sunrise, I wake up; I hear something moving. I quietly peek out the tent flap. A mother elephant and her three calves, small, medium, and large, are walking slowly nearby, heading directly toward my tent. I am over the moon with excitement! Surely they will turn away toward the meadow. But no—they keep coming toward me. My heart is racing. Will they really come to me? I can't even imagine it.

But they do. Slowly Mama walks up to my tent and, about ten feet away, deposits a steamy, gloppy, greenish-brown present on the ground. She then moves off and stands a very short distance away, munching on grass. The two older calves stay with her. But the baby comes directly to my tent. He playfully wraps his little trunk around a rope that supports the tent. I have to restrain myself from jumping up and down with glee. Will he reach inside the tent flap? What will he do if he finds this silly human hiding inside?

This moment is so precious that the photographer in me needs to record it. I can't help myself. However, as I move toward my camera, the noise is a bit much for the elephants. As the African sun slowly rises in the chill morning sky, they all walk off slowly, including Junior, out into the meadow and away.

When I finally recover my breath and my mind registers what just happened, I am dumbstruck with awe, reverence, and gratitude. This is my very last morning in Masai Mara. My beloved friends have come to say goodbye.

CHAPTER 5

HEARTS, TRUNKS, AND FEET

Today we share with you our hearts.

We have large hearts—not just physically, but emotionally as well. Because we feel deeply, we emote strongly. For example, you might witness this in the way we bond with one another, or how we grieve the death of one of ours. But it can also show up as anger, such as when elephants destroy things or attack people. It is especially prevalent in musth[2] bulls, who can be extraordinarily dangerous and destructive.

---

2   Musth is a state of heightened aggression that occurs during the rutting season, or heightened sexuality, in bull elephants. It can last for days to months.

Some people understand that animals do, in fact, have emotions—not so different from humans. In fact, we see that more and more people are realizing this.

What does this mean? It means that if people can see animals as emotional beings, with large hearts and a great capacity for love and sorrow, it will change the way they look at and treat us.

It is so easy for people to see you as "different." Traditionally, scientists were taught to avoid anthropomorphism, attributing human character-istics to animals. I certainly learned this while studying animal behavior. We were also taught to avoid any kind of emotional attachment to the animals we studied in order to stay "scientific." Fortunately, this is changing, but clearly not enough, from my perspective. It is easy to study you, write about you, paint you, photograph you, and keep you "out there" as beautiful beings without feelings. And these are the people who love you. What about the ones who don't?

As long as you keep us separate, you can do to us whatever you choose, without remorse. As soon as you see us as like you, part of you, you lose that distance and objectivity. And herein lies the conflict with science. Science is based on objectivity.

Yes, and now through quantum physics we are learning that even the act of watching something changes its behavior. So how objective can you be?

We do not attack science and scientists, animal lovers, or even animal haters here. That is not the idea. What we want is to get you to think about what you do and how you perceive.

I agree and I think this is really important. If a cow has feelings, how can you justify factory farming? If a lion has feelings, how can you justify putting it in a cage for the rest of its life? If a deer has feelings, how can you hunt it relentlessly so that it has no peace? If a gorilla has feelings, how can you send tourists to its home daily to watch its every behavior? If a whale has feelings, how can you surround it with twenty boats at a time? If a dolphin has feelings, how can you put it in a small tank and gawk at it? If a bear has feelings, how can you track it down and tree it with barking dogs? If a monkey has feel-ings, how can you put it in a tiny cage and traumatize it to conduct experiments? If a rabbit has feelings, how can you subject it to painful tests, just to see if eye makeup is harmful? If a mouse has feelings, how can you condemn thousands, even millions of them to lives of pain and suffering in the name of scientific research? If a chicken has feelings, how can you put it in a tiny pen and cut off its beak? And if a lobster has feelings, how can you put it in a tank with its body tied up so that it can't move?

This one-upmanship extends even to human beings. It is evident in the way men have treated women, whites have treated people of color, and in numerous other ways that human beings denigrate and abuse other people. So it is not just about the way animals are treated.

Exactly. The point we offer is that as long as people can see other beings as objects, without feelings or consciousness, there will be separation and disharmony, which leads to violence.

It is only, ONLY by elevating consciousness and awareness that this planet will survive with life as we know it. It is how we can move beyond the negativity that has been created and carried out. There is not time for anything else.

You do not have to get on a soapbox and preach. You cannot convert those whose minds are not open. All you can do is to give people willing to listen an opportunity to open their minds and hearts. That is all.

TRUNKS

We speak now about our trunks, those magical, multipurpose, incredible appendages that so deeply support us in all that we do. Because you have an entirely different reality, we will try to describe these trunks that are so much of who and what we are as elephants.

Our trunks are our tools, just like your hands are tools for you. We use them in a similar way. They are our primary means of interacting with the world. They may look strange to you because our form is so different from yours. But to us, you look strange! We are different, and that is what makes this conversation interesting and exciting. We can explain to you something of how we see the world.

We use our trunks to help us eat and drink water; quite obvious to any who observe us. What may not be as apparent is how our trunks can detect even minute changes in the atmosphere, in the attitude of other beings, in hormonal changes in those we interact with, or the scent of other species—whether they are allies or foes. So, in a sense, they are our antennae.

We use our trunks not only to spray water or dirt onto our own bodies, but to impart messages to others. Not just through sound, but also energetically. We can let other elephants know exactly who we are and what is our intent. Our trunks are a means of communication, a way of reaching out to others.

I am curious: do your trunks feel to you like our noses might feel to us? Like an extension of your face, but far longer than our human noses?

We don't have human noses so it is hard to say. But what we can say is that our trunks are indispensable to our bodies and simply feel like part of us. As would an eye or an ear. How would you feel if your nose were very long, and with that nose you could tell if someone were sincere, if the weather were about to change, if there were a threat to your well-being, if your long lost relative were close by, or if a catastrophe were about to occur? This is what our trunks can do. They are invaluable pieces of our anatomy that we treasure dearly.

Are they extremely sensitive, and even delicate in some ways?

Yes, of course. We can move them in a multitude of ways, in all directions, and they are quite strong. And yet, because of the delicate flaps on the end of our trunks, we can pick up small objects or relay intimate, sensitive messages through touch to our babies or those we love.

I have seen some elephants missing part of their trunks and yet they seem to survive. It must be challenging for them, like a person losing a limb.

Yes, much the same but, like you, we adjust. The capacity for healing and adapting is tremendous.

Is there anything else you want to tell me about this?

When we trumpet, or make other loud noises using our trunks, it is a wake up call for many beings. We let them know exactly who we are, where we are, and what we are feeling. This is another primal aspect to our trunks, exclusive to us, and incredibly important. Our trunks serve us well as we maneuver in a world that is becoming more and more complex and challenging.

THE TRUNK

An elephant trunk has about 40,000 muscles, while the entire human body only has about 650. It is a fusion of the nose and upper lip and is made up of about 150,000 sub-units of muscles. Babies don't know how to use their trunks when they are born, so it is a learning process. They are adorable as they try to use these trunks that flop around until they master control.

African elephants have two finger-like growths, called pro-boscides, at the tip of their trunks, while Asian elephants have one. These allow elephants extreme dexterity. They can pick up a single blade of grass or delicately wipe their eyes clean. At the same time, the trunk is strong. Elephants have been shown to lift up to 770 pounds with their trunks or pull up entire trees from the ground.

The long trunk allows an elephant to reach branches up to 20 feet high. It also serves as a snorkel in the water, so elephants can swim in deep water where other wildlife may not be able to.

Elephants have a keen sense of smell, believed to be four times that of a bloodhound. There are millions of chemical and olfactory receptor cells in the upper nasal cavities. The tip of the trunk contains two types of vibrissal hairs, small corpuscles and free nerve endings. These features can detect vibrations, allowing elephants to sense the rumble of far away herds or distant thunder.

FEET

Now we would like to talk about our feet. We have large feet and they support us well. But they are extremely sensitive. Even though they seem tough, the skin is easily damaged. Yes, we move about on all kinds of terrain and usually do quite well. We are used to this. But when we are put in captivity, especially on hard concrete, it is a different story. Our feet simply can't stand up to this kind of treatment. We were not meant to be on hard, unnatural ground. And so you will see that many of us in zoos, circuses, or other captive situations on abnormal substrates have foot problems.

Yes, I have seen this in zoos. Many elephants have nasty abscesses and penetrating wounds that require daily treatment. I am sure that can be invasive and uncomfortable. This is one of the many downsides of captivity and should never be allowed. But it is, and I am sorry.

Can you tell me anything about your feet when you live in a natural environment? I understand that they can make sounds that travel through the ground for long distances. Is this true? And if so, what is the purpose?

As you know, we are massive creatures and so our feet must support a lot of body weight. They are like pillars that hold us up. When we walk, these pillars impact the Earth in a powerful way. As they hit the ground, they produce sounds that travel through the medium on which we walk. Usually this is dry land. But it can be on muddy or wet environments. In any case, the impact of heavy legs and feet hitting the ground creates a wave of energy that moves through that habitat.

We didn't ask for this. It is just part of the package of these huge bodies. But there is great benefit to this process. The sound is carried in the earth for long distances. Other elephants sense this and know where we are, even who we are. They can tell how many of us there are in one area. They can sense if there are young ones among us. So this is a message to other elephants, relaying information that, in some cases, can be critically important.

Why is it important?

We often roam vast distances to get to our destinations. Sometimes there are conflicts between different family groups. Or there may be musth bulls we need to know about so we can be cautious or be prepared for mating. We then know what to expect. We can tell the direction they are traveling and can either avoid other elephants or go to meet them.

How can you know if they are friends or foes? Can you tell that from their footfalls?

Energy travels through the earth. If an elephant, or a group of elephants, is in a heightened state of excitement or anxiety, we can sense this from the signals that come to us through the ground. If the group is calm, we anticipate no trouble. But if, for instance, a bull is in an aggressive frame of mind or a family is agitated and fearful, we can feel that. Then we know what to expect and we can stay on course or move out of the way.

This is interesting and amazing. Most humans have no idea just how intricate your world really is. Is there anything else you want to tell me?

Yes. We can sense the presence of humans in this way as well, but from a much shorter distance. You don't have the same impact we do. But we feel things you would not be aware of.

If you can sense upset and aggressive humans, why wouldn't you just stay away? I know that many elephants raid crops, trample places, and even kill people. What is this about?

We are emotional creatures. When our homes and our food source have been taken from us, we can get hungry and angry. We may not be in control of our behavior. Imagine being with your family and finding that others have invaded your home and taken away all your food. Would you not be angry and frustrated? And, what if those people were also hateful and aggressive toward you? Wouldn't you respond in kind?

Of course I would. This is terrible. I can see how drastically your lives have been disrupted in many cases. I only hope that people will come to their senses and figure out ways to live together in harmony. I know at times it seems impossible, but if people can really, truly know who you are, maybe some day there will be peace and understanding. I can only hope and pray for that.

THE FEET

It has been scientifically shown that the footsteps of elephants transmit low frequency sound vibrations, called infrasounds, below the range of human hearing.

Elephants seem to be able to detect what are called seismic vibrations, or Rayleigh waves, in two ways. One is through dozens of touch receptors in the foot, called Pacinian corpuscles, that detect vibrations and send signals to the brain. The tip of the trunk also contains these corpuscles.

Experiments carried out by Dr. Caitlin O'Connell of Stanford University and her colleagues have shown that elephants can pick up these seismic signals and then orient in the direction of the vibrations and respond accordingly. These seismic signals seem to be detectable up to twenty miles away. Synchronized freezing is a common behavior when elephants in the wild detect something that alerts them to danger. Dr. O'Connell found that bulls will often lay their trunks on the ground when freezing, most likely to detect vibrations in the earth. [1]

The other way that elephants sense Rayleigh waves is through their bones. Scientists think seismic ground vibrations travel up from their feet, through their skeletons, to their ears. In this way, the vibrations are heard as well as felt.

So, when an agitated elephant stomps, he may be warning other elephants miles away. Or a musth male may detect the presence of females in the distance by sensing the vibrations made by their footfalls.

Other animals produce infrasonic calls as well, including whales, rhinoceroses, giraffes, and alligators, among others. Infrasound, with subsequent Rayleigh waves, is also produced by volcanoes, earthquakes, avalanches, and tsunamis.

Elephants detected the tsunami in Asia in 2004 long before humans did and were able to save themselves and people as well. The influence of electromagnetic waves may also have been a factor.

---

1   For more information, see her book, *The Elephants' Secret Sense.*

REFLECTIONS ON HEARTS, TRUNKS, AND FEET

Writing this chapter was huge for me. It was called Hearts and Trunks in my first book. After doing some editing, it seemed a little short so I asked the Elephants if they had anything to add. They wanted to talk about their feet. Okay. Seemed a bit strange, but I just let them speak. What they told me was amazing and completely changed something inside of me.

I have been working this way with Elephants for many years. I started writing my first book 20 years ago, in 2002, following a trip to Africa. I had been communicating with animals, including Elephants, for 5–10 years before that. Even so, with all this, I still doubted my work. I still questioned whether it really was the Elephants speaking to me, or just my mind making things up. I had no proof, other than reading about something that validated what they had told me. This actually happened on a number of occasions.

When they spoke about their feet being sensitive and susceptible to wounding, that wasn't surprising. I have been in zoos and know that elephants have a lot of foot issues. That wasn't really all that new. But when they shared about detecting information from the ground vibrations sent from other elephants, and how specific that information is, that was new. I hadn't heard anything like that before. I knew that Dr. Caitlin O'Connell had research showing that elephants transmit infrasonic sound waves through their feet. The Elephants had told me this long before I learned about her work. But I didn't know much more than that.

I was fascinated when the Elephants said they can determine where other elephants are, approximately how far away, how many, and if there are babies with them. It seemed so amazing that I wanted to see if I could learn more about how they do this. So I researched online.

What I found was that scientists have proven that elephants send and receive these infrasonic messages through the ground. This is called seismic transmission, and the sound vibrations create Rayleigh waves. I had no idea that these even existed. And then I read about Pacinian corpuscles in their feet that detect these sound waves, and that elephants have been seen many times by scientists to stop, listen, and turn toward the direction where the sound vibration comes from. Also, they can determine what kind of source it comes from—whether it is another elephant or an earthquake, for instance. It is not a stretch to assume they can detect a lone elephant or a herd making the sounds, or how far away they are.

This completely validated the information the Elephants had shared with me. Science proved what I was receiving. It shouldn't be a big revelation. After all, I have been doing this a very long time. But somehow it really registered this time. Now I know, without a doubt, that the Elephants are talking to me. What an honor this is, that they trust me with this kind of information. And I realize, even more, just how magnificent they are.

CHAPTER 6

MIGRATION

I know you navigate over large distances to find water and food, on trails used by elephants for thousands of years. How do you know where to go? Is it through ancient memories passed down from generation to generation? Do you have other means of migrating?

When we traverse great distances, as we often do, we use all our senses to help us navigate. We are complex beings and have many sensory systems we incorporate into this process. Yes, we follow ancient routes that have been laid down by our ancestors. But it is not that simple. There are obstacles. Many, in fact. And we use our intellect and acquired wisdom as we go. Often trails we follow have been obstructed by human interference or impediments placed by natural causes. We cannot count on any migration route being easy or direct.

So what do we use? We use our memories instilled by our mothers, grandmothers, and previous generations. They laid out a path before us that we do our best to follow. But we do not simply use landmarks and memory. We follow the sun as well. We utilize the path of the sun to help us navigate. It is an innate tool within us.

And more than this, we use our perception of energy. Energy of this kind is undetectable to most humans so it may be hard for you to understand or make sense of. When we trek over land, hundreds or thousands of times, our energy embeds itself in the very ground we walk upon. We sense this as we move forward and it helps keep us on track.

Sometimes these ancient trails are blocked by human settlements, fences, floods, or fires. In these cases we need to be creative and find different routes. This is where our intellect comes into play. Our matriarchs, whom we usually trust implicitly, gather all their strength, courage, and wisdom to guide us. Occasionally a matriarch shirks her duty or gets frightened and can't function. In that case, we do our best to replace her or utilize other elephants who may be calmer and have a better idea of what to do and where to go. It may even become a herd decision. But mostly our matriarch is our leader and we put our faith in her.

Do you also use the moon and stars?

At times, but more often we travel during the day using the sun. Predators are out at night and can more easily capture one of our babies if we are on the move.

CHINA ODYSSEY

In June 2021, I contacted the elephants that were walking across China. They had left their nature reserve and were heading north, making international news as they raided farms and residences, including a retirement home, while searching for food. Here is that conversation:

I call for the Souls of the 15 wild elephants that are trekking across China. I have watched videos and read reports about you and I would like to know what is happening from your perspective. Can you please tell me why you left the reserve and where you are going? It seems that the area where you lived has gotten much smaller and there may not

be space or food enough for you. Is this true? Are you simply looking for a new location or is there more to this?

As you have learned, there is a biodiversity conference happening here soon. This has not gone unnoticed by us. We are far more aware of things than what people can imagine. So this is all well orchestrated.

Ostensibly, yes, we are looking for a good place to live and we continue to move across this land until we find a new home. And, in the process, many people are becoming aware of our presence. China has been a huge market for tusks and other animal products in a harmful, damaging way. It is a travesty. But now we are right here, letting people know we exist and we have rights. We deserve to live. We deserve to be protected. And we deserve to be respected and honored. That is what is happening now. People are having to pay attention. We are not simply some foreign object to be used and abused, exploited, killed, and completely dishonored.

I get it and I know this is not an easy journey for you, especially with babies present. I also know that you have done some damage to crops and homes along the way. Is this your intention or just happenstance?

Of course, we do not intend to harm anyone or anything. But when things get in our way, we bust through them. We are too large to do otherwise. And we are curious. So we look into houses or cars or anything else in our way. AND we need food.

Do you have a destination in mind or are you just walking?

We know there are clear open spaces on the other side of this country. We feel it and know it. So we are heading in that direction. China has become so saturated with people that it is impossible to live here as a wild elephant. Therefore, we are searching for a place where we can raise our families in peace.

At the same time, as we have already stated, we have a message to deliver and we are drawing attention to it. It is that we, as wild animals, need to be respected, and allowed to live meaningful lives without the threat of needless harm. Many Chinese people have taken on the terrible mentality of killing other creatures for their own use without understanding the consequences. This needs to change and we are doing our best to make that happen.

I wish you all the best and I do hope you find your new home and can stay safe along the way. Is there anything else you want to say?

Yes, dear friend. Yes.

As you know, many animals are being harmed around the world. People have become completely disengaged from the natural world and think they own this planet. Anything or anyone that does not suit their needs is excess baggage. This cannot continue. The Earth cannot sustain this type of mentality and activity. If it goes on, we will all suffer and perhaps become extinct—including, of course, humans. We play one small role in delivering this message. We only hope that others will receive it and take positive action. Thank you for asking.

Thank you. I love you and I so applaud what you are doing.

I have one more question. I understand that a mother and her newborn baby and maybe another female have turned back. Is this true and, if so, why? I imagine it is because this journey is too hard for a young baby and they are going back to where there is a safe place and food to eat.

Exactly right. A mother will do all she can to protect her baby and she needs help. We are a community based animal. Family is everything. So she decided, rightly so, to turn back and take care of her young family.

This was written in June 2021, when these elephants were widely publicized around the world. After that, they seem to have disappeared from the media. The last I could find about them was in August of that year. At that time, they had wandered for over 17 months, more than 700 kilometers away from their reserve in Yunnan province.

An emergency committee was formed to herd them back to the reserve, using fences, bait, and fake roadways. Authorities cut power supplies to prevent the elephants from electrocuting themselves and sent police to evacuate roads and distract them from densely populated areas.

In August it was reported that 14 elephants were returning to the nature reserve from where they had come.

Asian elephants face the threat of extinction and have been given China's A-level state protection for wildlife. Most are found in Yunnan province.

CHAPTER 7

BULLS AND MATRIARCHS SPEAK

BULLS

As I sat with a group of male elephants in Africa, I perceived them as strong, powerful, and peaceful. It was such a tremendous gift to sense their presence with me. It fascinates me that you can be so calm and loving, and then shift into a state of heightened aggression during musth. It seems to be true of many animals, including humans, that males fight for dominance and "ownership" of females.

Many human women are rebelling against this. Our society is a patriarchy that often denigrates, dominates, and abuses women. For eons, this patriarchal attitude has led to wars and violence. Many of us pray for peace, and try to bring in more nurturing and compassionate feminine energy, in order to eradicate this madness.

And here you are, demonstrating two sides of male energy. Is there anything you can tell me about this?

We, as male elephants, or bulls, as you call us, embody the full range of emotion, from gentle being to formidable warrior. You cannot have one without the other. This is something that many people do not see. They think that if the human world were made up of only peace-loving, gentle souls, there would be peace and harmony. But it is not so, from our point of view.

Dual energies are in all of us that represent the polarity on Earth at this time. In everyone, there exists gentle, loving, peaceful energy as well as creative/destructive, aggressive, violent energy. To deny one is to deny the other. You may call aggression "the shadow" if you like. The truth is, it exists, and to deny it or ignore it is to cause disharmony in the self.

We act this out, often very dramatically. There are those in your society who do this as well. The problem arises when this energy is not channeled properly, or is not subdued when necessary. The raging tyrants get a strong hold on others and create havoc. In our world, we do become antagonistic and destructive when in musth. Others know to leave us alone. We used to have great spaces in which to roam, so others could avoid us.

Often, we choose to be alone at this time. As we come into musth, all the negative emotion we have harbored as a collective is dispelled. We do this for the group, by acting out the anger, frustration, and misery we all feel. It is a release of energy, not just for us alone, but for the herd.

In your world, because so many people are fighting their own inner natures and struggle just to survive in a violent world, they often feel they don't have an outlet for their feelings.

Yes, and so they busy themselves with mundane matters or live vicariously through actors or athletes to channel the energy. And the males in modern society, when they come of age and the hormones rage, what is their outlet? Sex? Violence? They are no different from you. The Maasai and other indigenous cultures of the world know this. They channel the adolescent, testosterone-laden energy into a period of time in the bush, tests of bravery, and sitting with wise elders to learn the ways of men. Where I live, we do not have this, and our culture suffers greatly.

We are loving. And yet, sometimes we need to act out these powerful emotions. It is our way. It is what must be.

As I hear your words, I realize your message seems very important. I wonder about the vision we share, in which all beings live in peace, love, and harmony. How does this relate to the need to express our anger and frustration, and the issue of pent-up hostility? How can we channel this energy appropriately, in a healthy and productive way?

It is not our place to tell each human how to live his or her life. There are many wise people who can help with this. What we can do is to paint a picture for you, and give you some guidelines, from our perspective.

We see a world in which people are rushing. Always in a hurry: to get somewhere, to do something, to outdo one another, to simply survive in a fast-paced world. It seems you need to slow down and take the time to find your balance again. It is only in stillness that we can find our own way.

We see that many humans are angry; they yell at one another, honk their horns, and channel this energy into frantic, frenetic activity. Eventually, some become violent.

We know anger. We feel it and we express it, sometimes not wisely. But for the most part, we grant one another the space to let it out. We pull down trees, spar with one another, trumpet, and chase each other in play. All of these are ways to release energy. We see that you are often too defined in your roles, too rigid in your expression, too lazy to move, or too complacent to act. The anger grows inside until it cannot help but express itself in some way.

Use elephants as an example, if you choose, of how to best express these feelings. It is absolutely necessary for us, and we see that it is for you as well.

I get your message and yet something seems missing here. When I asked how to channel this energy appropriately, I didn't get a very clear answer. When people are in the depths of anger and aggression, how can they just calm down, get quiet, and redirect that energy? As with musth bulls, it seems there is no recourse other than to remove themselves from others they might harm. Can this aggressive, highly charged energy actually be controlled somehow? How can people benefit from your wisdom and experience?

First, we want you, as a woman, to see that male energy can be quite dramatic. We know this occurs in human women as well, but not usually to the same degree as in many men, so for you, as a woman, to understand what we are saying may be a little difficult. Please try to put yourself in our position.

When our hormones rage, we are overtaken by a highly charged, fierce energy. We are inclined to mate or fight. It is hard to focus on anything else. It is actually not a very comfortable energy to live with. We are constantly on alert and easily angered and frustrated. But it is part of our nature and we have learned to deal with it.

The problem arises when we are confined in any way and can't move about. We need to move this energy out somehow, preferably in vast open spaces. Because our lands have been taken over by humans and fences, it is hard to escape, and so some of us become violent with people or other animals. It is unfortunate. At this time we are truly unable to fully control our own behavior.

So what does this have to do with humans? What do you see?

Humans do not seem to have the same hormone surges as we do. Maybe some men do, but most do not. It is a steadier process. Adolescent human males may be different. They have heightened levels of hormones and often act out. Much like our young bulls, those not well supervised or disciplined can get carried away with aggression.

We do not have a clear answer for men in your culture. But we can say that men, with their intellect, can take charge and control their behavior *if* they are open and willing. Many are not. Men not willing to take responsibility for their actions can hurt others, or themselves.

As humans, you have the capacity for great things. You can harness your strong minds and use your energy in useful rather than destructive ways. It is a matter of choice. Many people have been harmed throughout their lives and have not healed their wounds, so they are susceptible to reenacting the damage inflicted upon them. It is sad. But with healing, awareness, and positive intent, much of this violence can be eliminated. We hope that it can be so, before humans destroy all the good they have achieved.

As elephants, we ask to have space to move about and we ask for understanding on the part of humans. Let us be who we are. Find ways to live with us so no one gets harmed. This is all we ask.

What about the other side of your behavior, the calm, gentle side?

Once the hormone surge is over, we go back to our gentler nature; for us, a far easier state in which to be. We can rest and find companionship with other bulls or spend time on our own.

Why don't bulls associate with cows most of the time? It seems that the cows have beautiful family lives, but the bulls do not. What is that about?

We didn't create our lives, we simply live them. And this is what we know, what we do. It is our natural state of being.

MATRIARCHS

To me, you, as matriarchs, are magnificent. Is there anything you would like to share with me? I feel myself coming to a place of peace as I tap into your wise, loving presence. It seems that you embody that peace.

Peace comes from confidence. That is what we hold for the group. Without it, we would be lost.

Confidence, to us, means making decisions clearly, being fully loving even when things don't seem so loving, and being stable enough to stay calm even when things get out of control. To stay centered through the storms of life.

What then is the difference between peace and confidence?

Not much, from our perspective, so we almost use them synonymously. Peace comes from confidence; when you are sure of yourself, and when you treat others as equals, there is no need for anything other than peace and calm. Perhaps you wish to reflect on this awhile. It seems it does not register fully within you.

This is true. For me, peace and confidence have been separate concepts, but I am intrigued. I want to know how to find this confidence and peace. Can you tell me?

Yes. It is simple. When you let go of your fears and know that, whatever you do, wherever you go, everything is all right, you can come to a place of peace. There will be times when things seem miserable and chaotic. It is during these times that the greatest challenges occur. If you can know that no matter what, you and your loved ones will be all right, you can remain steady in a place of peace and confidence. You can know that no matter what, you are always exactly where you need to be, and that whatever happens is as it should be. This is divine acceptance.

This sounds great, but when you say that you will be "all right," what does that mean? You could get sick, be in harm's way, or die. So how can you say that you will be "all right" given these possibilities?

We see a much higher picture, a higher plan, if you like. You may not be all right in your physical, earthly existence. Your life could be in serious danger, or ones you love could be taken from you. This is part of living on Earth. But when you consider the divine plan, a higher purpose for all, it gives you a sense of relaxation and relief. Just knowing that this physical life is not all there is, that we go on as Souls in other realms, evolving as we go and enjoying our journey, can give you a true sense of peace. Surrendering to life and knowing that truly all is well. We are always guided and supported.

In the physical body, this awareness may not be apparent or even accessible. We can get rattled and lose our way. But ultimately, and this is especially the job of the lead matriarch, we find our way back to ourselves and that inner knowing that gives us reassurance. Then we can settle into a peaceful state.

What do you do if there is a threat to the herd? How do you make your decisions about what to do, knowing that your lives and the rest of the herd's lives are at stake?

We see what is happening first, so we know our options. We assess the situation, relying upon our instincts and our intuition, and then we act.

We move as we are directed. We don't question this knowledge. We know it comes from a place we may not understand. It is a combination of the wisdom of our ancestors, our own innate wisdom, our previous experiences, and the intelligence of the group.

I have learned that not all matriarchs are alike. Each has her own personality. Some are more fearful or aggressive than others. Scientists who have studied elephants have learned that the most successful matriarchs, in keeping their families alive and safe, know how to appropriately respond to each situation. I think of matriarchs as all wise and knowing, but maybe this is not always the case. Can you speak to this?

We are not so different from humans. We each have our own characters and tendencies. Perhaps by speaking as groups here: Bulls, Matriarchs, and Elephants in general, we give the impression that we are all alike, but this is far from true. We are individuals, just as you are.

Some of us are wiser than others. Some are stronger, some more gentle. Some fearful, some courageous. But what we all have in common is our love for our families and a passionate intention to protect the ones we love. We do our best. It is all we can do.

CHAPTER 8

RENEWING AN ANCIENT BOND

Long ago, humans and animals lived together in peace and harmony. We all understood how to share our world, and knew that each of us depended upon one another. We learned to cooperate and use our resources in a sustainable way. We spoke the same language, a language of the heart: of empathy, love, and compassion.

To you this may seem to be ancient history, well beyond what you as humans can remember. But we remember it well, in our blood and in our bones.

In those days, when we were one voice, one heart, we worked together for the betterment of the planet —not in tangible, physical ways, but spiritually. We attuned to the same rhythm. Life was simple then, without too many encumbrances. Because of this, it was easy to be silent, to listen to Spirit.

Over time, life became more complicated in your human world. Now things are shifting dramatically and drastically. Our world is changing, too, as a result of yours. Humans are powerful, and all the changes occurring for humankind create changes for all beings on this planet. Many of these shifts are destructive. It is for this reason we appeal to you to speak for us.

I can't stop crying. Something is registering so deep in me that I won't deny my calling to put these writings out to the world. I have doubted myself for so long. I can't do it any more. [3]

During the time when we were all one living, breathing, pulsing Spirit, our entire existence was interconnected. For this reason, when one harmed another being, all beings felt harmed. People and all other creatures knew this and avoided hurting others as much as possible. That has changed.

As humans began to assert their power in the world, their egos developed, which led to injustice and self-centered greed. Human desire for power often took over all sense of logic and reason.

Because animals have no capacity to change the world in the way humans do, we do not relate to this type of greed and passion for power. We are what we are. We do what we do. We live as we have lived for millennia, without a need to control.

You say you have no desire for power or control, so what is territoriality about? Do you not do your best to keep others out of your place? Is this not an attempt to control others?

A good point that we will clarify. It is true that we compete with one another and claim territories. This may appear like a desire for power and control. We see this. We do not imply that we are superior to humans in any way.

The scale of our territoriality and competition is different. We cannot rule the world; we do not have that capacity. We live in our small habitat and focus on making our lives better. We do not think about overtaking something outside our immediate range of awareness.

Greed is another matter. Greed is wanting more than what is

---

3   For me, tears are a sign that I am connecting deeply with something or someone. It is a signal that I have touched my deepest truth. It is also a response to a feeling of great love and support. So often, during the course of writing this book, tears came. Sometimes I mention it in writing, to acknowledge a deep place of connection with the animals, resonating with what they say.

sufficient for your own well-being. This does not have any role in our consciousness.

Thank you. This makes sense. I see that competition, when taken to an extreme, can lead to greed and manipulation. This is the attitude that initiates a conquering mentality and paves the way for wars and senseless violence.

Our deepest desire is to relay some idea of the relationship we once had with humanity in order to restore it. It may seem impossible, and logically it is not possible. The world is a far different place now. But one thing you and many others are learning is that logic and reason do not rule the world.

What does rule the world, if logic and reason do not?

Logic and reason are a means of understanding and making sense of the world, or so it seems. What is actually true is that Spirit, Source Energy, or Divine Consciousness rules the world. Everything else is a manifestation, a vehicle to carry out the orders of Spirit[4]. Control is an illusion. As long as human beings assume they can control what is, they will be disappointed and continually seek more control. The paradox is, when they are willing to relinquish control and surrender to Spirit, all things will work out exactly as they need to, regardless of their plan or agenda.

You can do your best to make changes, to make the world a better place, but ultimately, if you do not work in conjunction with Spirit, you will accomplish nothing.

This makes sense to me. So, how can we restore our ancient connection and live in a more peaceful world?

Long ago, when our ancestors roamed the Earth, life was simple. For many animals, the law was "eat or be eaten." For us, it was "'survive simply to survive." There were no agendas or complications.

How can you say that we lived in harmony and peace when animals were killing and eating other animals, even back then? This seems a contradiction to me.

---

4   Throughout this book, the word "God" is used synonymously with Spirit, All that Is, Universal Consciousness, Source, Creator, and is not associated here with any specific religious belief.

Earth is a school for spiritual evolution. Some lessons are not easy. Because of the planet's polarity, great contrast is part of the evolutionary system. If all were happy and peaceful, there would be little growth. So animals have been designed to kill and eat one another—that is until, or if, an evolutionary shift creates a new reality.

When we say we lived in peace with one another, that does not preclude predation or territoriality. It means we honored one another, accepted life as it was given, and had mutual respect for one another. If a prey animal was killed and eaten by another animal, there was spiritual agreement before the act was committed. This still holds true today, unless someone is so disconnected from their own soul essence that they ignore the spiritual rules. Many humans do.

Does this answer your question?

Yes. What happens to an animal when hunted by an unconscious human who kills with no prayer, blessing, or remorse?

That animal lets go of the body in a state of shock and may require assistance from those on the "other side" to heal the trauma.

Not a pretty picture. I hope people will become more conscious of who animals are and what human beings do to them. Please go on.

As the Earth and her inhabitants evolved, things became more convoluted. Interactions between species got more involved. The more types of animals and plants that existed, the more sophisticated the interactions. Our repertory of behaviors became more complex and with this, so did our thoughts and emotions. You can see the evolution of thought and awareness. In the human world it can be called intelligence. But it is more than that. It involves an expanded consciousness as well.

I am not getting this. I am caught up in the words. Can you simplify?

When one lives in a world of survival, life is simple. There is no time for deep expansive thinking. Emotions come up, but they are not analyzed or even given much attention. They are simply tools used to help one escape danger, to procreate, or to perform other basic functions.

But when one interacts with other life forms, the mechanisms of behavior and thinking need to be a lot more complex. It is not any longer simply a matter of kill or be killed. It is a question of, "How can

I interact with this being in a way that creates harmony for both of us, since we share the same environment?"

This is not necessarily a conscious thought process; it requires a higher level of intellectual functioning and more neurological pathways. And so we discover the evolution of intelligence, a wider repertory of behaviors, more intricate relationships, and creative problem solving.

If you had worked with our ancestors many years ago, you would have received different information. It certainly would not have been at this depth. The evolution of the soul—of an individual or a group—is a process.

Where are we going with this?

It seems that you feel your life is too complicated. The lives of many humans have gotten this way. Much information and stimulation come in now that were not present even in recent history.

You humans often think this stimulation is only about you. It is not. You are a piece of the consciousness of this planet. Your wonderful inventions and creations are gifts to you from the Universe, or God, if you choose to call it that. This is what is meant by co-creation: people open to receiving get inspiration and information and, at the same time, use their own wills, minds, and spirits to create new and wondrous things.

Your world becomes more and more complicated each day. Some of this is your doing, and some of it is handed to you. You cannot separate the forces. What people don't realize is that, like yours, our world is far more complex than it used to be. We are subject to the same forces and influences that you are.

Please continue our discussion about reestablishing our ancient connection with one another.

In the time when we were all intimately connected, there was an ease of communication, a sense of communion, and an exchange of wisdom and knowledge. For this reason, all beings learned from one another and shared their hearts and souls with each other. Because of this, there was no loneliness.

Loneliness seems to be a common disease in the modern human world. The connections between people have diminished or even disappeared in some societies. The relationship with the natural world—animals, plants, rocks, waters, all nature beings, and the Earth herself—is, in some cases, almost nonexistent. And so there is a great loneliness of spirit for many people.

This is true, at least in the more "developed" societies. People often move far from their homes of origin, and may live a great distance from those they love. They may live alone. It is no wonder people become so disconnected, lonely, and even angry and violent. There is no network to hold them when they feel sad, no one to nurture them when they feel lonely, no one to share in their triumphs and joys, and no reasonable outlet for anger or frustration. Sometimes there is no one to help the children, such as mentors who have learned from their own elders' wisdom. And so the cycle continues.

Yes. We hope to help you break the cycle for yourself and for others who can listen to and follow their heart's guidance. We know it is a tall order. Yet it is nothing extraordinary or even very exciting. It is simply looking at the world a little differently; a change in perception. That is all.

There is, in fact, a way to bring back the old relationship with self and others, which has all but disappeared in the current way of thinking and being. The way is through peace. Peace of mind, peace of spirit, peace between people, and peace with all beings.

How is that peace achieved? Not through struggle. Not through intellect. Not through trying to make anything happen. Peace simply IS. It is your nature. It is who you are, who we all are.

What does "peace" mean, and how do I find it?

Peace is a state of being where one is totally at home and comfortable with who she is and with what is happening in the universe. It is acceptance. It is love without judgment. It is harmony between all aspects of oneself and all others. It is our essential nature. It is how we live in the spirit world, if we don't take the woes and concerns of this world with us. It is who and what God, or Creative Force, intended us to be.

There are many ways to find peace. We offer peace through quiet connection, with us, with all nature spirits, and with anything that lives as part of the natural world. This does not always include companion animals, because they are often influenced by the people with whom they live. That is their function. It does not even include some captive animals or domesticated plants, because they do the same thing. It is those who are less influenced by the mind and attitudes of humankind who retain this type of peaceful awareness.

When peace is desired, it is important to stay connected to the natural world, which, for many, has become difficult to do. Your world is fraught with busy, frenetic energy and a struggle to get things done and "make a living." But what is "living" really about? Is it stress and strain? Or is it the peace you desperately seek?

You suggest connecting with the natural world in order to find peace. But isn't peace our true nature? Why do we have to go outside to find it? I certainly feel peace when I am in nature, but I know that peace comes from inside. How does a spiritual connection with you or a walk in nature facilitate this inner peace?

Of course, that peace is inside. We do not cause anything to happen, or give you anything you don't already have. We simply allow peace to come forth, through our great love and acceptance of you. By being with us at a deep level, you tap into universal forces. Peace is one of those forces. It is inherent within you, and when you connect with something that retains that sense of peace—whether it is an animal, a plant, a place, or even an object—your own inner peace is expanded and you simply become aware of it. The outer object, individual, or place does not give you peace. It is simply that by connecting with something larger than yourself, you are able to lose a sense of confinement and restriction and become the larger energy of peace that always exists. Does this make sense to you?

Yes. I have heard it said that it is possible to become addicted to nature, to form an attachment to being in nature—or attachment to anything that gives pleasure—and then lose yourself in that rather than sustaining yourself from the inside, where true peace resides. I would love to inhabit that peace all the time, even when I am in a chaotic or uncomfortable environment. I can't talk to Elephants constantly or be in wilderness all the time, so how do I maintain this sense of peace?

This is a great question. You do not need to talk with us in order to feel peace. But it is a way in. It is a beginning. The more you become accustomed to experiencing a feeling of peace, the easier it is to go there on your own. As we said, there are many ways to access peace. We offer one. Meditation is one. Being in nature is another. Doing something joyful can be a way in. Releasing sorrow or other challenging emotions can take you there. There are many paths. The hope is, the ultimate goal is, to live in peace always. And this is very possible; it requires exploring your own inner nature and connecting deeply with all that is peace.

This sounds simple and we know it is not, especially for people in such a busy world. However, with diligence, practice, commitment, and love—for self and others—it can be done.

ALLOW peace to take you over. There is nothing to DO other than allow what is already present to be expressed and felt.

CHAPTER 9

ELEPHANTS AND HUMANS LIVING TOGETHER

What causes conflict between elephants and humans and how can it be mitigated?

We have already spoken about our strong emotional nature and how, if not given enough space, we may express those emotions and do harm to others. In situations where elephants and people live together, sharing the same land and resources, it is difficult for us to have the space—physically, emotionally, and spiritually—to live within our own areas in a peaceful way. We are encroached upon by the expansion of agriculture and livestock farms. We cannot walk in many places without crossing roads, with cars impeding our way. We feel like our homes have been taken from us.

I am so sorry this is happening to you.

We do understand the human need for expansion, due to your rapid population growth. We don't blame humankind for what is happening. On the other hand, it is difficult for us to maintain our communities and territories in a peaceful way. Many of us are frustrated and angry.

You see, dear friend, on a spiritual level, as we are with you here, we are peaceful, calm, and wise. We do our best to accept what is and live with that. But in a physical reality, where emotions predominate, it is not so simple.

We have mentioned already that bulls in musth need room; otherwise, they can do a great deal of damage. They simply do what they feel the urge to do, which is often violent action. Cows, too, may have powerful emotions and can't help but express their feelings. If humans, water pipes, or other impediments seem to be the cause of our frustration and anger, they may be attacked.

There is a way to live in harmony and we (meaning elephants and people) must explore this together if any change is to occur. It cannot be one-sided. So in that vein, we wish to give you some suggestions. None is "the solution" that will end all this violence and fear, but it is a start.

We are sensitive to energy and emotions, so ending the cycle of fear and violence is important. When fear is sensed by a passing elephant, it is absorbed into her consciousness. We do not smell fear and then decide to attack. Rather, we feel the emotion which becomes part of our own consciousness, especially if the seed of fear is already there.

This reminds me of a story I heard about elephants raiding people's fields in Africa. A man and woman tried to shoo the elephants away. An elephant went after the woman and seemed to deliberately try to pick her up and throw her, eventually succeeding. The woman was severely injured.

This evidently happens regularly. It seems this woman did nothing but try to help her husband stop the elephants from raiding their crops. The elephants reacted violently. Is there anything that will stop this behavior? Not only is it harmful to people, but it also hurts elephants' chances of survival.

We are not always aligned with Spirit or in our highest state of awareness. Sometimes we react rather than respond consciously to a situation. So do not judge us as a whole by these acts.

Elephants and people have survived together for centuries. Both love and frustration have existed in this relationship. But now, as our habitat is taken away, we have no place to go. It may appear to humans that there is space available, but the truth is we are conditioned to live in certain areas. It may seem that these areas are no different from others surrounding them; however, this is not so. The energetics of a place can be more important than topography. If you take one place from us and expect us to live in another, it will not always happen readily or easily.

In the case of this woman, we do not know the story. But we suspect it was not as simple as it sounds. Perhaps there was a history of antagonism on both sides which escalated into violence. You ask what can be done to solve the problem of crop-raiding. It seems an impossible situation. People need a place to live. Likewise, elephants need a place to live. So when we encounter one another, there is bound to be conflict.

In this example, the woman likely sensed the elephants nearby and her fear was immediately activated. She was afraid her crops would be destroyed and she would be attacked.

What was she projecting to those elephants? She was creating a picture and an emotion in the elephants that matched her own. If these elephants were already frustrated and uncomfortable with the situation, her projection would lock into their anger and move them toward violence. Hence, the cycle is continued.

Let us imagine instead that this woman truly loves elephants and welcomes them to her home. She puts out some ears of corn as an offering. She blesses the animals, feels their pain at having their homes demolished and apologizes for peoples' ignorance and the sad state of overpopulation. She lets the elephants know that she does her best to survive in harmony with all beings and that she would appreciate it if the elephants would stay out of her fields.

What do you think the elephants perceive from this? Love, compassion, empathy, and acceptance. This energy, too, will tap into energy and emotions that exist in the elephants but has been suppressed. Her attitude will generate an atmosphere of peace and harmonious coexistence.

This is not to say that even under these circumstances the elephants will not raid her crops. We cannot guarantee this. Even if this lone woman stands firm in her love and compassion, perhaps others nearby project the energy of anger and fear, which may override her kindness. Unfortunately, this is reality. We wish it could be otherwise.

If a person does her best to be loving, it does not assure the best results. But it is essential to do it anyway. And as more people adopt this attitude, more elephants will be drawn into this beautiful energy. Like everything else, it takes time.

This problem does exist and people must take precautions to ensure their own safety. Strong fences may repel some elephants, but an angry elephant might charge the fence, just as he would charge anything that stands in the way.

I have heard about elephants figuring out how to get through electric fences. In some countries, people successfully use cayenne plants or bees as repellents to keep elephants away from crops. Your suggestion of changing attitudes to solve this problem seems too simplistic and unrealistic.

How do you fight anger? How do you alleviate frustration? Barriers, like handcuffs or jail cells, will keep people from doing what they have an urge to do, but it will not solve the problem. It is the same with fences or other deterrents. Shooting animals or distracting them with air guns and BB shots is also a form of barrier. It adds to the cycle of anger and violence.

The only way to really solve the problem is to raise consciousness. The only true long-lasting way to "fight" violence is with love and understanding. This is a tough issue in a place where there is long-standing conflict. Resources are dwindling while populations rise. But we tell you this, without reservation: if people will learn to truly honor elephants, and all living beings, as fellow spiritual partners, the resentment and hostility will disappear.

How is this accomplished? Through education. Through protection. If people knew they were protected by a person well-acquainted with elephants and their ways, the people would not need to fear. People who love and know elephants can teach others how to live with elephants. This is the way knowledge grows, and the way changes will be made.

CO-EXISTENCE

Can you say more about humans and elephants coexisting? How can we make this work?

The question of human/elephant interaction is enormous; each place, community, or habitat has its own concerns. Each situation is different. There is not one blanket answer to cover it all.

The idea of changing attitudes holds true wherever there is conflict. This is probably the most difficult and complicated of all solutions, but in the end, it is what will work long-term.

We cannot give you guidelines about how to change people's attitudes. What we can say is that it starts with children, who are most willing and open to learning. Adults are often set in their ways.

How do you teach children to love animals, when they see their parents battling us for survival? A tough question, and we do not have easy answers. We go through this within our own kind. There are many of us who are frustrated and angry because so much has been taken from us. The young ones grow up in this environment.

You have heard it said that solutions do not come from the same mindset that created the problems in the first place. And so to imagine that people and elephants can come to harmony and understanding from the same perspective that created the disharmony is not realistic. A whole new perspective is necessary: one that sees other beings, human or elephant, as equal partners. We need to live together. If we don't, we will all die.

Can you explain this? Why will humans die if elephants are gone? And why will elephants die if humans are gone?

We may not die physically, but we would die to the unfolding reality we are currently living. We help hold the energy of the Earth together, balanced and stabilized. Without this influence, chaos and turmoil could ensue. In time, big changes would occur that would certainly affect humankind.

Humans carry a different energy. You are the conscious creators. Without humans, the Earth would revert, over time, to a pristine state.

What's wrong with that? It sounds great to me!

There might be paradise on Earth, but spiritual growth could be greatly curtailed. We could survive here quite well without humans; however, you add a dimension to this reality that nothing else can. You bring new life, new creativity, new ideas, new beauty, new problems, and new solutions to this planet. Nothing else has this capacity.

So the evolution of the Earth and her inhabitants depends greatly on you and your choices.

Okay. I think I get it. So how do we live together? How do we teach the children to honor and love you, rather than fear and hate you?

Through compassion, understanding, and experience. Through sharing and communication.

Sounds great—but not so easy. And what about immediate concerns? What about the people who have their crops destroyed by elephants? How do we teach these people to love you? They are in survival mode, just as you are.

We have no easy answers or clear solutions, but we can give you our perspective. It is up to each individual to live his own life. We cannot make those decisions. If you understand how we see it, perhaps it will help give some clarity.

First of all, we do not hate humans. We understand. We do, however, get angry and may react from that place. It is not comfortable, and is not the highest response, but this is reality. And it is the same for humans. There will be those who want to destroy us.

And so it is up to us all to find ways to live together. Our land is being taken away. The freedom we once knew is long gone. This is a sad fact. The truth is, humans are taking over the world and we are left with nowhere to go. The interactions we have are colored with this reality.

This makes me so sad. It hurts me deeply to think that we, as a species, are destroying this planet. There is not much time left. Unless we all wake up, I think the world, as we know it, is not going to survive. And, unfortunately, all other life forms may go with us.

I apologize for my kind. I am so sorry. Not all of us are locked in greed, as you know. But many are, and I often feel hopeless. And I see that the human race is becoming so overpopulated that there doesn't seem to be any solution. It is a sad state of affairs. So when we speak about these issues, I have a hard time being optimistic.

We'll address this now. We sense your sadness. We feel it, too. But we also see possibilities you haven't even considered. If, indeed, we are all one consciousness, as we know we are, then we can solve this together. We have one common goal, and we are connected deeply with universal consciousness. The Universe is wise. We as beings living on this planet, cannot know everything. But our souls do. Our consciousness does. This is what we must reflect upon and turn to for help.

The human population *is* out of control; so is ours in some areas. In others, we are dying out. Why do you think this is? Do you believe this is happening with no spiritual purpose?

I have never thought about it that way. Of course, there must be a purpose. It seems that everything has a purpose, but I don't know what it is in this case.

Our point of view may open your mind and your heart to new possibilities. We see that overall your numbers are expanding and exploding, and ours are declining. This may be happening in order for all of us to pull together to find answers. This global problem requires great compassion and wisdom in order to be solved. As long as we remain separate, fearful, angry, and hopeless, nothing will happen. But if we realize that we are in this together and we can work together, great things can manifest.

Sounds wonderful. But what can we do?

There are programs to relocate elephants from overpopulated areas to areas where our numbers are minimal. This requires money and effort. Money and resources can be available, but greed often gets in the way, primarily because of corrupt leaders. We need to find a way to bypass this and get the money into the hands of caring people to continue this work. This is one solution.

As for your human population, this is up to you to solve. We see that greed, anger, lack of understanding and communication, and hopelessness keep people from moving forward. The ones in power care only about themselves and their personal needs. It is up to the general population to stand up and not allow this to continue. If your leaders were visionaries and were compassionate and conscious, your resources would be devoted to solving world problems rather than destroying one another.

HOPE

There is hope for us all. At the same time, we realize that time grows short. If it turns out that none of us survive, this is all right, too. We become Spirit once again, without these physical vehicles. It would be a shame that we have wasted this precious gift of the Earth that was given to us, but so be it. We will survive. We will go on to create new worlds, and hopefully we will learn something valuable from this experience. This is how we see it.

I hope there is a way we can all pull together. I would not want to be here without you and other species. I can't even imagine a world without nature. It seems horrific.

It seems critically important to open ourselves to a greater reality. I know that as one person becomes more conscious, an opening is created for others to become more conscious as well. That is simply how it works. So thank you for this message of hope. It gives me strength and courage to keep going.

We appreciate anyone who is willing to go to the depths in order to come to full conscious awareness. It is what will save us all.

I am aware of the disruption of your culture and all the violence that ensues as a result. There is some discussion now about post-traumatic stress syndrome in wild and captive elephants. Is your culture disappearing? Are young rogue males without male role models destroying your way of life? Have there been so many deaths, as a result of culling and poaching, that there is no sense of family any longer? Is the anger overtaking your entire society?

If you look at us from a purely physical perspective, our lives seem hopeless. Anger abounds. Loss of habitat is an everyday reality. Our lives have been severely disrupted by the presence of humankind. We are squeezed into smaller and smaller areas, even as our population grows in some places. In other areas, we are killed or exploited. So it does seem hopeless—as does your world, by the way. It is not so different.

With you, and those who are open enough to read this book, we choose to look at this issue from a higher perspective. We do not want to go to the mundane, dark, difficult places where most people go when speaking or writing about elephants.

It is true that our culture is suffering greatly from what occurs in our physical world today, in large part as a result of human influence.

It is a sad story, if you choose to focus here. But we see it differently.

We want to create a new reality and new perspective that perhaps takes us away from this harsh and seemingly hopeless viewpoint so prevalent on this planet. We envision a new way.

As we see it, the *only* way to change reality is from a higher perspective—meaning more aligned with Spirit or God or Higher Consciousness. And from this place of love and peace, to envision and create a different way of being on planet Earth. A way that honors all beings. A way that respects each individual's right to exist and to thrive. A way that works with others for the common good. A way that sees the welfare of the whole as more significant than the temporary satisfaction of the individual.

From 1992 to 1997, adolescent orphaned male elephants that had been introduced to Pilanesberg National Park in South Africa came into premature musth, a temporary state of heightened aggression and sexual activity. When females rejected their advances, the young males took their aggression out on endangered white rhinos, killing more than 40. Six older bull elephants, from a relatively normal Kruger Park population, were introduced to the park. The younger males' musth subsided and the rhino killing stopped.

In this book, we do not focus on what is wrong but rather on what we hope to achieve by coming from a higher place. There are no easy, quick solutions. The solutions to all the ills on this planet can only be solved from a consciousness different from that in which they arose. And this is what we portray in these writings.

It seems that elephants are becoming more and more aggressive with one another, other animals, and toward people. I know you are feeling lost and displaced and that you have strong emotions, as physical beings. I know you are suffering right now on this planet.

I want to know what is really going on from your perspective and how we can help, as caring people.

Our world, as we know it, is disintegrating and it scares us. We are, as you know, emotional creatures and we react strongly to things that bother us. And this bothers us in a big way.

What you *can* do, dear friend, is to love us and spread the word about who we are. And others can do the same. Sending prayers is magnificent. Connecting with us spiritually is sublime. Loving us is heaven for us. Anything else is less than elevating.

Do what you can to educate people. Do what you can to protect us and the people who live with us. Influence politicians and other people in power to help us rather than destroy us. This is all wonderful, beautiful, helpful.

But it must be accompanied by the deeper, more lasting, more effective work, in the spiritual realm. By connecting with us, loving us, and feeling our love for you, you shift the energy of negativity into one of love and forward momentum. And then, in the end, no matter what happens to us physically, we will all be healed and whole, loving and healthy.

Even if you cannot change the course of events that eliminates us from this planet, you *can* love us, know us, and be with us in profound ways. In that is the healing.

We pray that you truly understand this in your heart of hearts, for when you do, your life will change. No more worry. No more sadness. No more fear or even anger. Simply acceptance and love, for all beings and for self.

What could possibly be better than this?

THE SHIFT

You speak over and over again about how a shift in consciousness is all that will save humanity and possibly other life forms on this planet. Yes, great. But you don't speak much about how to do that.

I have seen too many people on the "spiritual path" who still live with a lot of negativity and old dysfunctional patterns and attitudes.

So spiritual practice alone isn't necessarily the path to love and compassion. People often still hold a great deal of anger, fear, and even hatred while elevating themselves to another realm where all seems beautiful and peaceful. But we are in bodies, here now. So how can we become loving, peaceful people?

This is a great question and we are glad you asked. We have mentioned "the shadow," especially when the Bulls spoke about musth and how they energetically hold space to express uncomfortable emotions for the herd.

But it is not just the Bulls that work with the darker emotions, "the shadow." We all, Elephants and Humans alike, are involved with this process.

It is one thing to transcend and connect with your higher nature, essentially leaving the planet for a time. In difficult situations, this can be lifesaving. However, in everyday life, it can be addictive and even dangerous. We live in bodies. We need to honor those bodies and function well within them. It is the same for humans.

I think this is called "spiritual bypass," when someone does spiritual work without taking responsibility for their own emotions and actions.

Whatever you call it, this can be harmful for the person as well as for others. To fail to acknowledge that you are in a body living on the Earth is deeply damaging. And extremely unproductive. There is work to be done here and "bypassing" it or ignoring it will eventually catch up with a person.

In what way?

Think about this: suppose you are in a constant state of meditation and, perhaps, bliss. This is all you want to do because it feels so good. Not all that different from being on drugs. You want more and more and, ultimately, you ignore the rest of your life. You may have trouble meeting your needs. You may spiral downward when, for some reason, you aren't able to meditate or connect in this way. And, potentially, you don't take action on behalf of anyone or anything else. You can become self-absorbed and inaccessible.

Certainly, when we speak of the need for humanity to be in a higher state of consciousness, we do not infer that people leave their bodies in any way. To heal this planet, work needs to be done. Not only spiritual work but physical work as well. We emphasize the importance of spiritual practice because when someone is consciously in tune with their own soul nature and higher guidance, they will be inspired to take appropriate action.

And what about emotional healing? Isn't that just as important as spiritual practice? I have found that when someone tries to communicate with animals or any other being telepathically, energetically, if they are

not clear about their own emotional blocks and resistances, they easily project those onto the subject of their communication. It is not healthy or beneficial for anyone.

Agreed. Completely. It is important to take responsibility for one's own mental and emotional health before attempting to relate to another being in this manner. Emotional healing is critically important if one wants to do any kind of meaningful spiritual work.

Thank you. And is there anything else we, humans, can do to heal our planet and our relationship with you and other species?

Honesty and integrity are key. To be authentic to your own nature is essential if you are to work with animals, and all other beings. We sense it when you are not.

CHAPTER 10

ELEPHANTS IN CAPTIVITY: ZOOS, CIRCUSES, AND THE ENTERTAINMENT INDUSTRY

Can you please speak about elephants in captive situations, living in cages—especially in zoos, circuses, roadside zoos, and amusement parks? I know it is a different story for elephants in legitimate sanctuaries where they are treated well.

Yes, of course. This is true. We are treated well in some zoos, but that is a completely different situation from a sanctuary, given the nature of most zoos. Zoos are commercial enterprises, based on earning money by using elephants as entertainment. The primary goal of legitimate sanctuaries is our welfare.

We, as elephants, require companionship of our own kind. We live in family groups with close attachments, and associate with other elephants in larger groups. Our relationships are everything to us, as is our need to roam free in large areas.

When we are put in a cage or other enclosure, particularly alone, we may experience extreme trauma. And it's worse if we have been taken from our home and family. It is not in our nature to live this way.

From our perspective, there are several stages an animal may go through when put in a cage. First is fear and terror. She just wants OUT! There is no thought involved, simply an instinctive survival response.

Once the animal realizes there is no escape, she may begin to settle down. Anger can well up. Fear certainly remains. And she may despair.

After awhile, something else occurs. It is as if the organism, geared to survival at any cost, realizes that the way to live in this situation is to give in.

Several things can happen. The animal may adapt to the situation and learn to survive in it, and even learn to dwell in a state of joy and inner freedom. You can see this in the way some animals act. They actually seem happy, and they very well may be.

But the animal may be overcome by sadness, pain, and rage, and may never leave this state. This is determined by the conditions under which she finds herself as well as the inner workings of the psyche. The animal may become nervous and agitated. You have seen animals who constantly pace and never seem to relax.

In other cases, she may become quiet and passive, and yet inside she is eaten up emotionally. She may succumb to some systemic break-down and eventually die of "dis-ease." Some animals may express their resentment and frustration by being aggressive and violent, like the lion who always snarls and growls at passers-by.

At least she is able to express herself to some degree so the emotions are not internalized as much. But it is a stressful and unhealthy way to live.

This is no different from humans in cages, which you call prisons. Some adapt, others do not.

I often have the feeling when I visit zoo elephants that they are bored and lonely, and sometimes frustrated and angry. Is this true, and what can be done about it?

When we are caged in a zoo, or worse yet, in a circus, we often suffer.

This situation is far removed from our true nature; we feel out of control, lonely, bored, stifled, and even hopeless in many cases.

Often, our only recourse to maintain some sense of sanity and dignity, is to leave our bodies, transcending our physical reality. Some elephants are better at it than others, but we all are born with this capacity. And if we are taught by our mothers and families, we can become more skilled at this than if we are orphaned or abandoned early on.

Another complicating factor is our sensitivity to taking on the emotions of others. If we live in a situation where we are surrounded by people, we may succumb to their emotions and their personal reality. In this case, we lose our sense of ourselves to some degree and become enmeshed in the consciousness of those around us. This is not a happy situation, particularly if we are held captive and are controlled by people who are not caring or kind, or who may have ill intent.

Even so, we are still elephants, and we can often maintain enough spiritual awareness to remove ourselves energetically, at least temporarily, from an unbearable situation.

We do suffer in captivity, and we implore humans to stop this terrible practice. All we are saying is that in some cases we can transcend the horror and the terror and reach into other realms.

I had a couple of interesting experiences with elephants in zoos years ago. The first time I went to the zoo, I experienced the elephants' pain and boredom. I stood close to them and cried, out of deep sadness. It wasn't helpful for them or for me.

The second time I went with a different attitude. I felt joy. I envisioned them as elephants in the wild, happy and free. This time I left feeling light and uplifted rather than sad, but the elephants didn't respond to me physically either time. Was this just me, in my own experience, or did I reach them at some level? Why didn't they respond to me at all?

Rather than feeling sad and angry for the elephants the second time, you saw them with loving eyes and a joyful open heart. That is the gift you brought them.

You were concerned because they made no effort to come to you or acknowledge your presence. You held a belief that if you are communicating telepathically with someone, they should somehow respond and give you a sign that they are listening. This is an ego call for proof that your work is effective.

Over and over again you have seen that this is not true. Animals rarely acknowledge you in this way. If you understand this dynamic, perhaps it will put your mind at ease.

When you speak telepathically with us or anyone, what does it really mean? What occurs? There is a merging of energy. It is as if you become one heart and soul with the being(s) with whom you communicate. You enter the consciousness of the other. You take on their reality—emotionally and experientially. You actually become the other, temporarily.

All this goes on at subtle levels of reality. You enter what some call "the dreamtime." As with a nighttime dream, your conscious mind may not be aware. This is why people can sleepwalk, or even talk while sleeping, and not remember it. The dreamtime and this physical reality are often quite separate. As you telepathically communicate with an animal, that animal goes on living its life in this current reality, not necessarily aware of what is going on in dreamtime. It is like two separate realities, or two distinct worlds, occurring simultaneously. Look at it this way: you are tapping into the unconscious—meaning a world that is not conscious. So why would the animal acknowledge you?

Depending on the animal, he may sense what you are doing and may be fully aware of your presence.

But this doesn't generally happen, especially with animals involved in other activities or emotional states.

The elephants at the zoo were eating when you were with them. That was their focus, and because they were so bored much of the time, they were not fully present, not aware of what was going on around them.

Do not base anything on animals' reactions to you and what you are doing. They may be receiving all you say or do and not show a single physical sign.

CAGES

Can you speak about caged animals in general? Is it always a spiritual choice for them to be caged? Why do some animals do well in cages and others do not? What are the lessons to be learned? What can we, as humans, do when we encounter caged animals, in order to be of service?

This is a big topic, but we are happy and even grateful to address it. You are absolutely right; some animals fare better than others in cages. Some cannot stand it and would rather die. In fact, many do die in cages. Others may live lives of misery and despair. And yet others seem to adapt just fine and live happy lives. What is the difference? What makes one cope and another not?

Part of it is attitude. Just as with human beings who create their own emotional cages, animals in cages can choose how to live within their situations. How many people do you know who are supposedly free and live blessed lives, and yet still create their own inner cages?

I have been one. Sometimes, even when it seems I had everything going for me, I was unhappy, and critical of myself and others. At those times I focused on what's wrong rather than what's right and I easily fell into frustration and despair. So I do understand about living in a cage of our own making.

And that is the point. It can be a choice. However, there are situations that are abominable and cannot be judged otherwise. In these situations, life can truly be miserable.

What makes one animal adjust and another not? It may be a matter of individual personality and personal history. It could be related to whether or not that animal's basic needs are met. It also depends on the attitudes of people and other animals involved in the situation. And, of course, if the situation is horrendous, it is hard to be happy. So there are many factors involved.

Do animals choose, on a soul level, to live in cages?

Probably not, for most.

This is distressing. Somehow I can accept a horrendous situation if I think it is a choice. But if it is not, how horrible is that?

We sense your pain and frustration at the cruelty of some people, and how so many suffer as a result. But there is more. Maybe this will help.

We are all here together in this experiment called life. No one knows the outcome. We are just testing the waters, sticking our feet in to see what happens—and then take the plunge if it feels good. Some of us are thrown in the water, head first, and need to swim or drown. For most of us, this is how it is. Sometimes life is challenging. If you let yourself feel the suffering of the world, it can be overwhelming. You cannot stay in this painful place long or you will die of despair.

But there is also incredible joy and lightness. The beauty of the natural world is astounding. The gifts that can be offered to one another are magnificent. The capacity we all have for sharing love and tenderness is enormous. And so, dear friend, there is a balance. That is what this planet is about, that balance of light and dark. Always teetering on the edge, trying to find that middle point where it all works.

We say that many animals in cages do not choose to be there, and yet there they are. Why? What meaning can we give it? What meaning can we give to the many people who starve each day? Or to the wars? Or the struggle of life and death that occurs in every moment? It is all the same question.

There is not one answer that will make life seem easy and simple. But what we can say is that each step honors one's spiritual evolution. You are put in a cage: what can you learn? Next time around, maybe you will be a little gentler. That is a soul level choice.

From other spiritual teachings, I learned about karma—the law of cause and effect. I had thought the soul chooses into which body and circumstance it will incarnate.

From our perspective and knowledge we, unlike humans, do not choose a specific time or place to incarnate. We choose lessons to learn, and you may call this karma. We choose to be with certain family members we know well and love. We may choose to learn about life in captivity and what that entails, but from what we are aware of, we do not choose an exact body or situation.

Why would you choose captivity?

It is part of our evolution, to know what it is like to be held captive by human beings, and then to either come to a place of acceptance and cooperation or to rebel. If it is a horrendous situation, we have to learn how to cope with it. These are big life lessons we are engaged in, just as humans have their own lessons that can be challenging.

We may choose situations that teach us compassion, patience, acceptance, and forgiveness. We direct our intent to that purpose. The rest is in God's hands to get us to the right place. So we don't really choose the place, per se, but we do choose the lesson to learn. All is by intent, not concrete choices.

We are not as analytical or rational as humans. Our lifestyle is more flexible and fluid. We do not think the way you do. We sense and know things, certainly, but we do not analyze or assess things. We simply act.

Even in the spirit realm, we make our choices and live with the consequences. We do not figure out exactly what particular animal we will become, which zoo we will drop into, or dwell on details of that particular life. We go there and trust that it is appropriate.

Does this mean you don't have freedom of choice? Some people believe that animals don't have this capacity, that only human beings do. It is also said by some that animals do not have individual souls, but only group souls.

Do you believe these things?

No. My relationship with animals, on a soul level, has been magnificent. I see little difference between the souls of animals and the souls of humans. I fully believe, feel, and know that there is no hierarchy of souls. That on a soul level we are all the same. All part of one great consciousness.

By seeing animals as "less than" humans, it keeps us subordinate. We become objects to be used. If you see us as fellow souls in different physical form, it gives you the responsibility to treat us with kindness, respect, and care.

Yes, I see how this is true. When human beings see other human beings as "less than," they feel justified in subordinating, exploiting, and abusing them. Similarly, when people think of animals as "less than," it seems to give them the right to do all kinds of awful things and feel justified, like cruel testing in labs, factory farming, puppy mills, killing animals ruthlessly for the products we can obtain, or putting a trophy on the wall.

Yes. But a very subtle degree of dishonoring animals occurs at the soul level. To believe that we do not have individual souls, that we act as part of a group without individual consciousness, makes us one step removed from you.

Because we do not produce what humans produce, or speak in human language, we can be seen as inferior. Humans use all kinds of testing methods to determine our intelligence. And when we are seen as smart, you can love us. If we fail your tests and are considered dumb, you don't have much interest. It is because the mind is given such importance in your way of thinking, believing, and viewing the world.

Our intelligence is more related to our lifestyles than the criteria with which human beings are familiar or comfortable. So, for us, intelligence tests created by humans are worthless. Look at who we are, how we live, what we do. This is our form of intelligence and wisdom.

We see what happens here on this planet as a grand experiment. A wondrous adventure. Some of it is fun and light. Some of it is very dark and difficult. Some animals suffer greatly at the hands of humans.

That is how it is. And just as humans have choices, so do we. We can choose to carry anger and frustration, or we can transcend and transform it, as long as the harm done to us is not too severe to overcome.

HELPFUL ACTION

What can we do to help animals in cages? Some radical animal rights people release animals from cages, but the animals are often so used to the cages they don't know what to do once released. What about animals in zoos or other places? Is there anything we can do as caring people?

There is a great deal you can do. It may seem insignificant because you probably won't notice any obvious changes in the animal's behavior or attitude, but on a spiritual level, any gesture you make toward helping that animal cope will be appreciated and integrated.

For instance, when you pass a caged animal in a zoo, acknowledge the animal in all its magnificence. Each animal has its own special qualities. He may be exquisitely beautiful. She may be unique or gifted in some way. He may be fascinating in his behavior or appearance.

There is always something. If you can recognize that and let the animal know you *see* her and *feel* her in her majesty, this alone will be of great benefit.

Have you seen people walk up to a cage and then laugh and tease an animal? Perhaps one time won't matter so much. But day after day, year after year, imagine the harm this does to an animal's sense of well-being. It is atrocious. Instead, send that animal love, appreciation, and gratitude. It will make a difference.

Once this connection has been made, there is more you can do. If you remain with that animal and tell him how sorry you are that he lives in a cage, he will understand and appreciate your empathy. But if you dwell on this, you will only increase his sadness.

Instead, focus on joy. Focus on being with that animal and the beauty you create together. See yourselves romping together in a field of flowers. See yourself hugging that animal and telling her how much you love her. See that animal wild and free, with her own family. Whatever you do, *feel* the love and joy, and send that clear message to the animal. It is the feeling, more than anything else, that will help her.

You can also relay to that animal your appreciation of what he does for the world by being in a cage. There is always a higher reason for that animal to be there. It may be serving as an ambassador for his species, to teach people how to love and appreciate another life form. It may be to help others in some way, or to serve as your personal messenger, to wake something in you that needs to be discovered. Acknowledge the gift the animal brings and send your deepest gratitude. This will be of great benefit to that animal.

And finally, if all else fails, cry.

I feel this. I felt tears stinging my eyes as you said this. What is it about?

Sometimes the most you can do for yourself or others is to express your feelings fully. If you put on a brave front and keep these painful emotions locked inside, it will eat you up. And, certainly, animals are sensitive to this. To try to hold a positive image for an animal in a cage while inside you are eaten up by sorrow will not help anyone. The best thing is to release it. The animal will feel it and bond with you even more. As you cry, you enable the animal to cry as well. We don't have tears as you do, but we have the same emotions.

This last part has touched me deeply. For years now I have known that to send negative emotions to a caged animal, or any animal in pain, only makes things worse. But I have seen that when I am immersed in my own sadness and pain and I can release it, animals often sense this and come near me. So this makes a lot of sense. There *is* tremendous sadness in the world. To deny it seems ridiculous. To feel it and then express it seems to release it. Thank you for this.

Is this, though, a contradiction to what you just said: to send joy and love to that animal and not negativity?

No. What we mean is that you need to release any emotion on the surface in order to be fully present with and available for that animal. Once you have cleared your mind and heart, then you can send positive, loving energy. But don't deny your true feelings. Animals will sense it and disconnect from you energetically. We are masters at sensing truth and authenticity.

DEALING WITH ABUSE

This is all sweet and great, but I know about the horrendous abuse of elephants in captivity. Even those considered to be premier zoos for elephants, like San Diego, Portland, and Seattle in the United States, have histories of elephant abuse. The beatings are unfathomable, and were condoned by government authorities in the past. It is shocking. Things are better now and still improving. Some zoos have a no contact policy with their elephants. Larger circuses can't operate with elephants as they used to. Many people are standing up on your behalf. Unfortunately, there are still backward places with people in charge who lack compassion. I find it so upsetting.

This has gone on for centuries, in every country where elephants are in captivity. It is horrendous. I ask you now for your help with this. You have told me that you can often transcend and remove yourselves from the situation to some degree. But there is pain and suffering that elephants endure. How do you stand it? Why do you even stay on this planet?

We love that you care so much, but getting distraught is not helpful for you or anyone else. It depletes your energy and makes you incapable of being fully supportive. So get a grip! You cannot allow yourself to get pulled down like this. Remember, life in a body on Earth is all temporary and there are other realities. This is one of many.

We are here to help humanity evolve. When humanity evolves, so does every other living thing on Earth. It is an energy revolution!

In the grand scheme of things, you are babies. Babies make mistakes. Babies are self-centered. Babies are afraid that someone else is going to take something from them so they become protective of what is "theirs." Babies have to learn and grow. They need to be taught and corrected when they do something wrong rather than being chastised.

So it is with humans. You are bound to make mistakes and let your egos take charge. You need to learn to care for others.

We understand this. In some ways, we are wiser. Yes, you have intelligence and abilities that we can't begin to master. But we know how life works. We know how to love and care for one another.

When you speak about the abuse we suffer, it is indeed a travesty. It is painful and distressing. Some of us become angry and can't control it. Others become passive and submit. This is how we survive in a harsh reality.

You ask why we stay. This assumes that we can leave our bodies at any time, but it is not true. Like you, we came with a mission and that mission overrides our own individual, self-based desires. So, although we might want to leave when we suffer greatly, it is not always an option. We stay and endure.

Overall, after the way you have been treated by humans, it seems that you are more forgiving and understanding than most humans. How do you do that?

Our nature is to love. Our mission is to support. This is how we survive. We reach our higher purpose and potential by honoring the contract made long before coming to Earth. It is what guides us and allows us to survive.

But certainly you must get angry when these horrible things happen to you. Don't you?

Yes. And, as we said, some of us can't control the anger and then go haywire. But most of us have learned to adapt. Some of us learn to love kind and generous people. At our core, we mean no harm, and unless harm is done to us, we are tolerant creatures. Of course, there are rogues, just as in any society or culture. But basically we are gentle and loving and we try to keep it that way.

Thank you for speaking with me about this.

And thank you for asking. Most people don't consider speaking with us. It helps us to talk about these things rather than keeping our feelings bottled up. So thank you for asking.

I feel calm now. Thank you. Thank you. Thank you.

CHAPTER 11

THE LOVE OF FAMILY

I would like to focus on joy now. There is so much heaviness and sadness in the world. Let's lighten this conversation up a bit!

We will speak of our babies. What could be more joyful than that?

When we give birth to a young one, the entire group is involved. We relish the experience. We all congratulate the mother, of course, and more than this, we share the responsibility as well as the joy of raising the baby and watching him grow and evolve. It is truly a pleasure to be with this new life and participate in his unfolding.

Our babies are precious to us: not only because they are beautiful and wondrous little beings, but because we know they hold all the blessings of the future. Each new generation holds different and more evolved consciousness. Each baby is the bearer of great wisdom, beyond what we have known before, because knowledge is passed from generation to generation through our blood and bones, and through our experiences. Each young one is the recipient of an entire universe of wisdom, discernment, and care. This is truly wonderful, if you think about it.

When a baby is born, she is greeted with great enthusiasm by all family members. The consciousness of that baby melds with that of the group. There is no separation. We act as individuals, with our own personalities and unique attributes, but our consciousness is closely linked with the others in the group; we often think and feel as one unit. The baby takes on group energy. As a result, this baby becomes us. What this means is that as we learn, grow, and act, the baby shares our experience. This is how she learns and evolves.

The baby comes complete in her spiritual makeup but has much to learn about living in a physical body. This is what we teach. At the same time, what we learn is profound. Each time a young one comes, she brings with her universal wisdom and the great teachings of others from thousands of years. It is all held within this little body.

This is not to say the elders do not contain this wisdom as well. Of course they do! But because they have lived on this Earth for so long, and have had so many earthly experiences, the spiritual wisdom is not on the surface as it is in the young ones. It is accessible and available, but some of the sparkle is gone. A sense of wonder and imagination is rekindled by the presence of an innocent and inexperienced baby.

The baby quickly becomes a member of the group and, as such, is cared for by all. When we move, he moves. If he doesn't, we find out why and help him. If he has a problem, it is our problem. If he plays joyfully, we all feel joy.

Thank you so much for the joy you impart. I can feel it. I do have a question, however. I have seen a film where a baby who was stuck in a mud hole was abandoned by the group. Only the mother remained to help her baby. What is this about?

Always, our preference is to support, protect, and care for our families and friends. We love one another and support each other, so to help our group members is important. However, there are occasions in which the benefit of the group must come before the welfare of an individual. The case you describe is one of those situations.

If the group is in danger because of the misfortune of one of our members, we may choose to leave that area. It is more important to protect the well-being of the entire herd than to save one or two individuals. If possible, we do all we can to stay with and support any elephant in trouble. But if we feel it is more important to move on than to assist a mother, we will do so.

Similarly, if a mother dies, perhaps killed by poachers, and leaves her baby behind, our first inclination is to care for that baby. However, if we feel that our lives may be endangered if we stay with this little one, we may find it necessary to leave, thus abandoning the baby. This is sad, but it is our reality.

As you know, when a baby is left, it will most likely die, unless we can return to her or humans take over her raising and care. Babies are like human babies in terms of their emotions and reliance on their mothers. They grieve deeply when their mother is taken away. We are grateful for the generosity and loving concern of humans who care for these lost babies; a service beyond our ability to repay. To these people we are truly grateful.

And so, dear friend, we hope that in some small way we have uplifted your heart through our sharing of this wondrous adventure of baby rearing. It is one of our greatest joys.

You have. Thank you so much.

LOVE

I feel bathed in a field of love as I sit with you. It is incredible. I feel so very blessed and grateful.

This feeling is what we live and embody, and you are receiving a taste of it.

We want to share with you something very dear to us; our relationship with our families and groups of friends.[5]

I feel something very deep and beautiful emerging in me. I have a lot of emotion coming up and it seems to be related somehow.

Because we have what you long for. There is something special, significant, loving, and warm about the relationships we have with one

---

5   Groups of elephants comprised of family groups are called bond groups.

another. Some people sense this and are drawn to us for this reason. They may not even know why they feel that connection, but if they search their hearts, they will find it. It is an interesting paradox for humans to consider us. On one hand, we are strong and large, and for many, we represent strength and power. Some people are drawn to our power and want to increase their own.

But our power does not come from physical size and strength alone. Our true power comes from the our relationships and our God-force, the power of the Universe. When we greet one another, there is great exuberance and joy. It is because we are truly delighted to be in the presence of another fellow Soul. We share our lives, our environment, our history, our reverence for life. And because of this, we never feel alone.

When you see an elephant in a zoo, circus, or any kind of captivity, who has been separated from her family, you are seeing a great tragedy.

Sometimes these animals can form new bonds, but they have shared such history of so many lifetimes with family members, there is often tremendous loneliness of spirit that cannot be resolved. These animals may become violent or depressed. If people understood the depth of our relationships, they might think and act differently toward us.

Yes, this is so cruel. Many people now are fighting to free elephants from these situations, but it is not enough. There are still far too many ignorant people who simply don't get it. I apologize for humanity's narrow-mindedness and selfishness. But please continue.

The lead elephant, the matriarch, is the holder of our world. She keeps us together, guides us, and offers us her great wisdom. And yet we do not see her as a spiritual leader and God-like. We honor her, we love her, we follow her, and yet we know spiritual power is within us all. A matriarch's role is to enable us to find our own way, while being guided and supported by the group.

You might not see this if you look at us from the surface. It is not evident because it looks as if we are all following the leader. We are, in a sense. However, our relationship goes far deeper than this. We are individual personalities and souls, held together by the power of the group.

It is hard to explain what kind of strength this gives us. It is a security you may not be able to understand; it seems that few humans truly experience it.

The power of the group is stabilizing, harmonizing, empowering, and loving. It gives us a feeling of security and well-being which allows us to feel a sense of freedom and love that is rare. We know this; we appreciate it greatly. We would like to share this with you and with others. If you can feel it, you can create it within yourself and in your life. That is one of our most precious gifts to you.

CHAPTER 12

ASIAN ELEPHANTS

I feel sad thinking about the work you do in Asia and how hard it must be. Elephants are often treated abusively. I know there are many caring people who rescue you and give you sanctuary, which is a great blessing. From what I understand, not many elephants work in the forests any longer. Often you work with your mahouts in town to earn money or entertain tourists. What a tragedy that is.

It is not easy being an elephant subjugated by humans. Although there are those here who treat us with kindness and understanding, many people, as in most of the world, do not understand our deepest nature. They might praise and honor us in their religious ceremonies, and yet when they work with us, hands-on, they often disrespect and exploit us for their own needs. It is an awkward situation. Some of us rebel; and, of course, we are badly mistreated in that case. There is no escape. We have two choices: tolerate the abuse and do our best to remain calm and civil, or rebel and suffer or die. Some choose the latter, but most of us choose the former.

For centuries we have served humanity in our own way. Humans have reviled us, worshipped us, abused us, elevated us, lived with us, died with us, misunderstood us, and communed with us in very profound ways. Together, ours is a long history of mixed blessings and crimes, love and hate, denial and acceptance.

When I asked the Elephants earlier about animals in cages, you, as part of the greater soul consciousness of Elephants, told me that you don't choose the abusive situation per se but you do choose to be here.

We choose to be here and to live this lifestyle, even though it is very difficult and painful at times, because our lives are intimately inter-twined with and dependent upon the ways of humans. This is our choice. This is our choice. This is our choice.

We say this to you, and repeat the message, because you must understand that we are not victims.

This touches me deeply. A lot of emotion is coming up, and I don't even know why.

Perhaps it is because you are in love with us, dear sister, and you now appreciate the gift we give humans.

It is true. I am so moved. Just as I was when chickens, cattle, and other "food animals" told me they sacrifice themselves for our nourishment, and all they want in return is a little respect and kindness. I was moved when the gorillas told me they are on display for tourists in the wild to teach people about who they are. And when dogs, cats, horses, and other companion animals, over and over again, tell me about the great sacrifices they make for the people they love. It is overwhelming to take in this kind of generosity and love.

I am humbled by this. I feel that anything I can do for you is nothing compared to what you offer humankind. My appreciation and gratitude cannot be expressed in words.

TSUNAMI

Many people have praised you for your courage, insight, and generos-ity during the tsunami in Asia in 2004. You were aware of the oncoming storm before most humans were, and I understand some of you took the initiative to save children and adults by carrying them away from the ocean when the tsunami hit. You were also involved in the clean-up operation. After all the abuse and suffering you have endured for so many years, why did you do it? How did you even know to do it?

You know us better than to think that we do not know what we do or to think that we are not compassionate, loving beings. Yes, sometimes we suffer; and at other times we are greatly loved and treated well. We know that the people we saved never did us any harm. They were simply people wanting to survive and we did all we could to help.

We are so much more in touch with the Earth and her vibrations than most people could ever be, due to the conditioning that removes them from the forces of nature. It was clear to us that a natural disaster was occurring and we did what we could to save ourselves and help others. It is not a mystery. It is simply what we were called to do, and we did it.

We love people. We do not especially favor those who harm us, but we do not condemn all of humanity because of the unconscious, unloving acts of some individuals. We continue to work with human beings as loving partners, as long as you or anyone else reaches out to us. This is our nature and our way.

Because of our relationship with people and our familiarity with and comfort in the rainforest, we were best suited to help with this clean-up effort. It was our honor, but not necessarily our pleasure. It was hard and tedious work, and often depressing. As you know, we have strong emotions that are easily triggered. At the same time, as we have shared with you, we can transcend this reality when necessary. It is our saving grace.

We did our work with pride and dignity. We were pleased we could help retrieve bodies, move debris, and reshape our world in this way. Many people died or suffered unimaginable losses; there was tremendous pain and suffering. It was truly a tragedy. If this were our only reality, we would not have been able to bear it.

Would you please say more about how you view the tsunami and other natural disasters, as well as people's relationship to these Earth changes?

Because you like metaphors and stories, we will give you one, and perhaps this will clarify it. A disaster is only seen as such by the ones who describe it this way. For others, these natural events may be experienced as positive changes. It is all a matter of perception. If your home is destroyed and your child is lost at sea, it is seen as a disaster. If you are far away from the storm, and new coastline is created with sandy beaches, you might see it as a blessing. This is a big part of what we want to relay to you and the readers: that all is simply a matter of perception.

Let us tell a story so that you might see, on a smaller scale, how this works.

There is a young boy named Banyu who lives on the coast of Indonesia. He fishes for his family and as a means to earn a living, just as his ancestors have done for generations. He is familiar with the sea and respects its wishes. He knows that when the strong winds come and the sea is a bubbling turmoil of water and waves, it is time to leave and go home. He knows that when the sea is calm, the creatures beneath the surface are docile and therefore easy to work with. He understands the ways of the water. He honors the consciousness of the ocean and all her wonderful creatures. He lives in harmony with his environment.

One day, a great wave overtakes his little boat. Unlike most storms, this one came up suddenly and has caught him unprepared, and with no time to go back to shore. And so his boat capsizes and Banyu is thrown overboard, into the raging sea.

What does Banyu do next? Because he is so attuned to the ocean and its ways, he does not panic. He knows he can survive if only he can remain calm. And so he grabs hold of his boat and finds the paddle, and then paddles himself to shore.

It is not an easy journey; the waves are huge and aggressive. It takes all his strength to hold onto his boat as he is swept under the surface over and over again. But he finally conquers the mad tumult and finds his way to shore, huffing and puffing, coughing and spitting out salt water.

Once he sets foot on shore, Banyu takes the time to thank the great Ocean Spirit for sparing his life. Why, you might ask, does he do this? It was through his own efforts that he was saved. The sea was about to do him in, had he not taken matters into his own hands and made his way to shore. So why thank the Ocean?

This is what we want you to see. The Ocean did not intentionally try to harm Banyu. It simply did what oceans do. It made waves and caused great chaotic energy with the aid of the wind. This is how things often change and release and grow: through tumultuous, violent, and what seems to be destructive energy.

Banyu knew this. He did not blame the ocean for his problems. He accepted what was and dealt with it. And the reason he thanked the Ocean was because he knew that without this kind of chaos, nothing new could be birthed. And he also knew that because he kept his head about him, he was able to survive a great challenge. He thanked the Ocean Spirit for teaching him this lesson and for helping him grow through courage and tenacity.

Had Banyu been an angry, vengeful person, he could have gotten angry at the sea for giving him no warning. Instead, he knew the ocean was not out to get him, that he was not a victim, and that his job, as a human being, was simply to work WITH the sea rather than fight it.

And so, in the end, Banyu's life was spared and he came out of this "disaster" a stronger person, and even more attuned to the consciousness of the Ocean. In the future, he will be much better able to predict a storm far in advance of its occurrence because his body has incorporated that awareness more than it had before this storm.

What does this have to do with tsunamis and other natural events? And why do you tell me this now?

We want you to see that people in Asia or anywhere else are like Banyu. There are millions of people who live by the sea. Some of these people are more conscious than others about the natural flow and are more attuned to the consciousness of the Earth and Oceans. But mostly, people are so far removed from natural rhythms that they are caught off guard when a storm hits.

The sea and the ones who live by and interact with it are one. Consciousness transcends individuality. And so, in the case of Banyu, his reverence for the Ocean and his union with it caused him to remain calm during the storm. This allowed the sea to penetrate his consciousness so he could work with it rather than against it, thus, saving his life.

This is not to say that his journey to shore was easy. Quite the contrary. The ocean did not part in order for him to reach the shore! But it was his deep connection with the forces of nature that gave him the courage, wisdom, and tenacity to survive. And not only to survive, but to learn and grow from his experience.

As Elephants, we feel this connection with the sea and the forces of nature, and for this reason we were able to escape the tsunami. We felt it coming.

On the other hand, people have been so disconnected from nature that most did not sense its approach, just as Banyu was caught off guard in the storm. And because they were so removed from the rhythms of the Earth, many of them panicked.

Our point is this: because people have been separated from nature for so long, and have given way to a consciousness of fear, victimization, anger, and betrayal, they have, for the most part, lost that great connection with the consciousness of Mother Earth. This disconnect, in turn, creates havoc and disparate energy. It is this disparate energy that contributes to the chaotic energy of a storm and can exacerbate the violence contained within. Not only this, but the disconnect can cause panic rather than the calm presence of mind that leads to appropriate, possibly life-saving action.

We would ask human beings to reexamine their relationship with the natural world. It is critical in these times of such great chaos in the natural world, as well as in the human-created world.

ACTS OF NATURE

The tsunami was not an act of nature designed to destroy and devastate. It was a natural occurrence as a result of the energy in the area; it allowed for a cleansing so that harmony could be restored in a new way.

Although humans are not directly responsible for acts of nature, they are a part of nature. They are not separate from it. All is connected.

The acts of humans affect the Earth, just as the happenings of the Earth affect humans. So people do not create storms, but they can greatly influence them. The tsunami in Asia was a natural occurrence. There was an earthquake big and powerful enough to affect a large area, exacerbated and intensified by the energy already present in this region. That energy was influenced and contributed to by human beings. Many people lived in this region and with them existed a certain energy; a result of the group consciousness.

If there is a consciousness of peace, love, well-being, harmony and acceptance, the energy of the area reflects this peace. Conversely, if there is a consciousness of fear, pain, and suffering, the energy of the region reflects this.

I understand. It has been shown now that water aligns with the energy that is imbued to it from the consciousness that engulfs it.[6]

So it is with all of nature: water, air, land, plants, animals, and minerals. If there is disharmony, the environment is saturated with discordant, turbulent energy. In time, this energy collects and forms a whirlwind, which then needs some place to go. If a storm is brewing, this energy can move into that storm and intensify it. If there is an earthquake, the energy can align with that as well. This is what happened in Asia. Does this make sense to you?

Yes. And what about tornadoes, fires, floods, and hurricanes all over the world? You cannot tell me that all of these are triggered or aggravated by human consciousness in a region, can you?

As we said earlier, human consciousness is part of nature. Because your minds are powerful and your numbers large, you greatly influence the physical world. Nature acts on its own, and yet the energy created by human intervention cannot be denied. This is a complex issue. Just as the thought, "You create your own reality" can lead to self-blame when there is illness, so the idea that acts of nature can be influenced by human consciousness seems like a judgment when not taken at the highest level. It is important to understand spiritual concepts from a non-judgmental and open place. This is what we ask of you now. No one was to blame for the tsunami, but we can learn its lessons. A sense of unity and love was created worldwide in support of the victims of this tragic event. May that sense of compassionate connection continue, without the need for devastating events to trigger it.

---

6   The research showing that water takes on and expresses the energy surrounding it can be found in *Messages from Water, Volumes 1, 2, and 3* and *The Hidden Messages in Water*– Masaru Emoto.

CHAPTER 13

CULLING, POACHING, AND HUNTING

I now realize that some of the ideas I was taught years ago by scientists and wildlife conservationists, such as using certain wildlife products in order to pay for conservation and to support local indigenous people, may be part of an old patriarchal system. It involves using animals as commodities: the animals are killed in order to sell their body parts. This promotes animals as something to be exploited and harmed, no matter what the result. Even if it is a positive outcome, the method is madness.

I was taught that culling elephants, a euphemism for killing, was necessary in order to preserve the land for elephants and other species. Elephants can destroy large tracts by knocking down trees and eating all the vegetation. It used to be that you, dear Elephants, would spend time in a place and then move to another, in order to give the land time to recover. But now, in many areas, that is not possible.

Still, it seems to me that killing elephants in the name of land preservation is absolutely wrong, inhumane, abusive, violent, and unnecessary. Many conservationists hold this perspective, while others do not.

So, what is the solution? Population control? I met a wildlife contraception expert who had been working with elephants in South Africa for years and he claimed great success. But others disagree. They say that contraception interferes with normal behavior in destructive ways.

How do you feel about contraception and culling? And if not these methods, what do you suggest?

How we see this situation may not make things any easier. It may not restore our habitat. But it is the truth as we know it.

We have lived with people for centuries now, both in Asia and Africa. Your focus is Africa because it is what you know, but there are elephants in Asia who work directly with people; our relationship with humans is different there. It is important that we make this distinction. So let's be clear that we are talking about Africa now.

Some believe it is in our best interest, and in the interest of other wildlife, to kill, or cull, elephants in numbers. They believe it logical to kill an entire family rather than one elephant at a time, particularly a matriarch or a mother. In this way fewer lives are affected, or so it might seem.

We do not see it this way. If any one of us is lost, it is a loss for all. That being is not recoverable or replaceable. And the death of entire families is tragic.

As elephants, our lives are interdependent. It may seem that we do not relate to one another out in the bush, but the truth is, we always know where other elephants are, and we live our lives accordingly. Even if we are not related by blood, or do not live in a cohesive group with other elephants, we know who they are, where they are, and what they are doing. Living our lives is based on this knowledge. When a large segment of our population is destroyed, we feel it. We feel the pain and the terror, and it affects us all deeply.

You may think we live through it, go on to have families, and return to life as it was. But this is not so. Our lives are changed forever each time one of us is harmed in any way. We feel it. We know it. And we are affected by it.

Yes, it seems that if a stranger is killed in a faraway place, it doesn't affect us so much, as humans. The news is full of horror stories every day. Our population is over seven billion now. Of course, we cannot be aware of each person who dies or is in pain. If we were, we couldn't live our own lives because we would be so overwhelmed emotionally.

But over time, as you deny the pain of others, you inflict deeper pain upon yourselves. You cannot live in this world and pretend to live alone. It doesn't work.

Our elephant population is smaller than your human population and is dwindling. We live a lifestyle closely connected with our community. We are deeply affected by the loss of any of our numbers.

The hurt, rage, and fear we experience passes directly to all other elephants. And, in time, those disturbing emotions are sometimes acted out in destructive ways that affect humans as well as other creatures.

Contraception is a good idea. Sometimes it works; it may keep us from overpopulating. But at a cost. There is a divine plan at work and, no matter how powerful humans think they are, they cannot override this plan. That plan calls for reproduction as a tool to maintain species survival. When the plan is interfered with, in any way, other checks and balances take over. So you may prevent a given female from producing a baby, but it throws off the way we interact with one another. We cannot know all the consequences.

I am disappointed that all of these methods have negative effects, and there seems to be no alternative. Do you have any suggestions?

First, we do not wish to discount all that humans have done on our behalf. There are many caring people working diligently to help protect us and make our lives better. We deeply appreciate these wonderful people.

Contraception may be a solution in some areas; again, we do not discount the value of this and other methods used to control our numbers. We are trying to bring people a different perspective altogether, one in which we co-create a totally new reality.

Humans have free will and intelligence. They have hands which enable them to do things other beings cannot. If they can learn to cooperate with the Universe, or God, or whatever you choose to call this force, they will co-create a better world for all beings. If they choose to go against the natural law, they will destroy what is here. It is very simple.

I would like more clarity about culling. Some people believe culling is necessary to preserve habitat while others say culling is done only for aesthetic and economic reasons and that it is not a true solution for anything.

From our perspective, the way culling is done is atrocious. People decide who to kill and who to spare; the results are devastating to us. We understand the need to limit our population, to sustain life on lands destroyed by our intervention. And we see that this dilemma is a heavy weight for many interested in our welfare and the welfare of other wildlife, and also for people who live off the land.

We cannot offer an easy solution. However, we do have a suggestion. It might never be followed; many people are not open to the idea that we have feelings, much less intellect and ideas. But we will give it to you anyway.

As you can communicate with us in this way, so can others. What if people were to simply ask us who is ready to go and who is not? We then could make a conscious choice.

Are you telling me that some animals are willing to die so others can live?

Yes.

Whole families?

Perhaps. More likely individuals.

But these people kill hundreds of elephants. Would there be that many volunteers?

Perhaps, yes, if the elephants truly understood.

I have a hard time believing or accepting this. The survival instinct is strong and elephants are so social that it seems one death is a tragedy to the herd. That is why people kill families now, so that the surviving family members will not have to live with this grief.

Think about this. If there were a disaster in your society and some people needed to die, would you prefer to have entire families killed?

Or would you rather ask if some would choose to die so that others could live? Think about how people feel about war. It's all right for men to die, but not women and children. Why? Because the children are the wellspring of new life. They are the future. Without them, all dies. And mothers are their caregivers and lifeblood.

Why would it be different with us? People think that by killing whole families they spare the rest of us, but this is not true. We are a big family; the death of any part of us is a death to something precious within our society. We are not dumb animals, unaware of what goes on around us. We are conscious, loving, feeling beings. We are connected to one another, as we are to the Earth. We do not destroy habitat because we are malicious. We do it to survive, and our survival has been limited by the intrusion of people. Perhaps it is up to you to find better solutions. One might be to ask us.

Another might be to provide us more land. Both seem unreasonable now, but in the future, when people are more conscious, hopefully, these will be viable options.

Your population, like ours, is taking over the world and destroying many habitats. Your survival is in jeopardy, just like ours. But you keep expanding. It seems there must be other solutions. And perhaps, if we work together on our common problems, we will find common solutions. Is it not worth a try?

Of course. I wish people could participate in conversations like this and actually ask you directly what you think and how you feel. But the vast majority of human beings are not ready for this. Certainly our leaders are not. My prayer is that the time will come, and soon, when interspecies conversations will be possible on a large scale, not just for a few of us. So, my friends, what about this? What can we do?

There is no easy answer. We have stated that, if given the choice, many of us would give our lives to save others. This even applies to others of different species, if we truly understood the severity of the situation and the repercussions. We do not ask you or anyone else to be the spokesperson for this. It would be too painful and wouldn't be accepted by authorities anyway. However, we did want you to know the truth of the situation.

POACHING

Poaching is also an issue. Large numbers of elephants are lost this way. Illegally slaughtering elephants is big business; the people at the top of the chain make enormous amounts of money selling tusks, especially to Asian markets. Some countries have taken measures to stop this practice, yet it continues. Can you speak about this from your point of view?

As you know, many calves become orphans because of poaching. These babies would die without the help of other family members or compassionate human beings who devote their lives to the care of these babies. We are grateful to them for what they do for us.

Some of our most beloved matriarchs, mothers, and bulls have been lost to us this way. It takes a huge toll on us emotionally, physically, socially, and psychically. Some of our young males have no role models and can become quite unruly, and even dangerous to other animals and to humans.

What can we say about poaching? There is not much, other than we wish human beings were aware of what they do and would end the pointless suffering and death they inflict on us and other living beings.

I am so very sorry that this is going on. Our only hope now lies with the concerned people who do their best to protect elephants and stop this horrific crime. More and more rangers, some with trained dogs, are in the field to protect you and other wildlife. We can only hope and pray that somehow you will be safe soon.

HUNTING

This brings up another closely related issue. People who hunt elephants; mostly the wealthy, who derive joy from killing elephants and placing a trophy on their wall. It is a "manly" thing to do. Hunting is still legal in some places. This is ridiculous and needs to be stopped. But again, money talks and greed speaks loudly. I apologize for these human shortcomings that allow this to continue. I know it is not enough, but I am so very sorry.

We do not hold you responsible, or the many others like you who truly care. We don't generalize about human beings, assuming you are all filled with ignorance and hatred. This ongoing tragedy hurts us deeply, and there is not much we can do about it, other than to stay away from certain people. But, often, there is no warning in advance.

Maybe this will help, to restate something we have talked about before: to us, death is not the frightening, terrible ordeal many people make it out to be. We know we leave these bodies and move into a realm of light, love, and peace. We honor the life we have been given and mourn those who have passed on. But we don't dwell on this different state of existence that we call death. We simply accept it and move on.

This reminds me of a vivid and clear vision I had some years ago that helped ease the grief and despair I felt due to the deaths of so many elephants at the hands of poachers. In this vision, I saw Elephants of Light, who had transitioned into the Spirit world, shining down on the Earth. I knew then that your lives are not lost in vain, that even out of body, you contribute to the well-being of all of us who remain embodied on our precious planet. Chapter 15 is the story of receiving this vision.

CHAPTER 14

PAIN, DEATH, AND TRANSCENDENCE

You have shared that when you experience fear or pain, you can transcend it and mentally leave your body. Can you please explain what this means?

When one of us, or even an entire group, is in a situation of great pain or terror, we can move beyond physical reality, or Earth consciousness, into a higher spiritual realm, where there is no pain or fear. We rest there, while simultaneously being present in the body. In this way, we don't focus on the discomfort. This is what might be called "transcendence."

We urge you to practice this. In fact, when you communicate with us, you are bridging two worlds. It is the same thing: being fully in your body, in physical presence, and being in the spiritual realm, tapping into universal consciousness.

Isn't it still possible to feel pain in this state?

It is a matter of perception and where you put your attention and focus. If you are deeply immersed in this communication process with us, or any situation where you move into another state of consciousness beyond the earthly realm, you may not notice your pain or negative emotions.

You are, in fact, transcending your earthly reality.

My concern when you say this is that people may take it to mean you don't suffer at all and therefore it is all right to harm you. That is the last thing I want to promote. Can you speak to this?

Of course, we suffer and feel pain. In fact, we are extremely sensitive. Besides having sensitive bodies, we are intelligent, insightful, and aware enough to know what is happening around us and to us. When we are hurt, we know it and feel it, just as you do.

We are saying that we, through generations of conditioning and training, have learned to access higher spiritual realms. At times, we can use this ability to focus there rather than on unhappy situations in which we find ourselves.

This does not eliminate pain or any kind of harm but helps us survive it. And it is temporary. We can't sustain this indefinitely. Some of us, those raised without mothers or other elephants to teach them, may not learn to do this.

Perhaps they have been more conditioned to human than to elephant ways of being and have lost this precious ability to move beyond current reality.

So you say that by confining elephants and separating them from their families, people not only deprive elephants of their freedom, but also may prevent them from using coping mechanisms to deal with the situation. That is truly sad; I hope people wake up enough to realize the harm they do.

We believe that most people, if they were aware of the damage they do by confining us, would stop the practice. That is our hope, and why we speak to you about this now.

GRIEF

I have seen films and read about elephants who closely examine the remains of elephants who have died. In Joyce Poole's beautiful book, *Coming of Age with Elephants: A Memoir,* she described how, when elephants come upon a dead elephant, or their remains, a ritual takes place. They get very quiet and continually touch the bones and tusks. They may spread leaves and dirt over the dead body, like a sacred ceremony. Can you describe what goes on?

We know that the spirit of an animal goes to another realm when the body dies and still has a conscious connection with the body. We have great compassion for the one who has died, particularly if it was a painful or traumatic death.

When we lose someone, we grieve, just like you do. It is no different. We may honor that one in our own way by covering them with natural items, such as leaves or dirt. The body eventually goes back into the Earth. Even if an animal is eaten by other animals, it all returns to the Earth. We honor this process. Symbolically, we cover the animal with parts of the Earth, knowing that this being will return to our Earth Mother.

When we encounter the bones and tusks of elephants long dead, we stop and pay homage. The bones and body parts contain more information than humans can sense. We can tell the approximate age, sex, and the particular characteristics of that animal simply by touch and smell.

By paying attention to that one's bones and tusks, we essentially call them in energetically in order to bless them, honor them, and appreciate them. The one who has died often comes to us spiritually to thank us and to be part of this ceremony. Then she departs, feeling consoled and supported, so she can move on to a higher state of consciousness. She is uplifted, in a sense, by the loving consideration of those left behind.

That is so sweet and beautiful. I wish more humans understood and honored death in this way. It seems that you may also stomp on or throw tusks during this time. What is that about?

Tusks, for us, are a symbol of power. They represent our strength, courage, tenacity, wisdom, and authority. We may treat the tusks more aggressively than the bones in order to honor these powerful characteristics. It requires a more vigorous kind of touch than what we use for the bones.

Is there a spiritual significance to this process of honoring death that goes beyond what you have described?

When we come upon an elephant who has died, whether recently or long ago, we want to establish a recognition of that being as one of us. We know that life goes on, beyond death of the body. That being is still alive in spirit form. By lovingly touching the body, we let that one know we acknowledge who and what they were, and still are. Their life has meaning. We establish a sense of kinship with that being which goes beyond mere physicality. It is a statement of our connection with the Divine. It is an acknowledgement and appreciation for life at its highest, most holy aspect.

I read in Dr. Poole's book that there have been cases of an elephant killing or injuring a person and then standing vigil over them, protecting them. What is that about?

As we have said, we are emotional creatures; sometimes our emotions win out and we have no control over them. We may reach out in anger or fear with acts of violence and aggression, and human beings can be the recipients. But once the anger has passed and we see what we have done, we feel deep regret.

We do not mean to hurt anyone. What we can do is protect that person by standing by and guarding their body, our way of honoring them and keeping the body from harm until they have made their full transition.

DEATH

We would like to speak with you about death; it is clearly an energy with you now. We see that you are deepening your relationship to death and the spirit world.

Yes, that's true. For example, during the movie called "Titanic," as I watched the ship sink, I saw people struggling to survive. It was a gruesome scene. Yet, is this any more gruesome than what happens in the world today, with wars, violence, and killing of elephants? In truth, it is no different.

If you can transcend the earthly connotations of death, you will live more freely and happily. We want to assist you with this.

The instinct to survive is born in all of us when we come to Earth. We all have this powerful force. Life wants to sustain itself.

When you fight for your life, it makes life more precious. If you gave it up easily, there would be less value to it and less appreciation for it. Struggling to survive makes you appreciate life more.

Is this true for animals, even those with little capacity for thought?

Yes. Anything that is hard won is more cherished. If everything were easy, life would be taken for granted and the beauty of it might be ignored. Even a little paramecium (a single-celled microscopic organism) exerts energy to survive. And in this exertion of energy, its life becomes more dear and valuable.

But isn't appreciation a thought process? Can paramecia think?

For humans, because you think, it is a thought process. For others, it is a feeling process. That which you struggle to keep, that which you fight for, that which you exert energy to have, becomes a precious commodity. Life has more meaning, even to those who cannot think.

This is very interesting. What does this have to do with me and other people?

As you are exposed to more and more people who die, you realize how precious your own life is. Because you can think and feel, you can embody the emotions that come with another person's struggle to survive as well as their release into death.

As a result of this process, your own life has more meaning. You take it more seriously. You reevaluate what is most important to you. You honor your own life as something significant and purposeful. You do not waste time or energy on things that do not matter. That is the value of being with others as they live out their own dying process. It becomes yours.

I get it. Thank you for this.

We wish to ask you this question: Once it really is time to die, the fight to live is meaningless. It is time to surrender. Why battle against death? Why not just give in and die when the time comes? Why is it so important to hold on so tightly to life? We see this happening with many humans, and it can be the source of great suffering.

I don't know, now that you mention it. It doesn't even make sense. Death isn't such a bad thing, after all, so why bother expending so much energy?

We encourage you to look at this carefully. Death is not a bad thing; it is simply a transition to another state of being, without the encumbrances of the body. We certainly view it this way. The fight to survive is helpful when there is hope. It is pointless and draining when the time comes to let go.

CHAPTER 15

ELEPHANTS IN THE SKY

It is a glorious, still, September evening. I am sitting at the top of Mt. Ashland, at 7000 feet elevation, waiting to contact ETs. Yes, extraterrestrials, those beings from other planets and star systems that are here to help us Earthlings evolve in consciousness. I think of them as Star Beings. This is far different from the media image of ETs as aliens trying to take over the world and destroy all in their path.

Who are these ETs? They are divine, benevolent beings who join us, invited by our strong and clear intention. They live in different dimensions and can take on energetic forms, although, from what I can sense, these are not the dense forms of Earth's physical reality. Other extraterrestrial beings may exist who are not so benevolent, but because of our clear invitation to these beings in particular, they are the ones who show up.

This is the evening of Yom Kippur, the holiest day of the Jewish year. It is the Day of Atonement, when Jews ask for forgiveness for their sins of the past year. I am Jewish and don't often go to religious services, but I do honor the sanctity of the high holy days with my own practice of prayer, meditation, and contemplation. This day has been a quiet, introspective day for me and I am still in that place of reverence and depth.

There are nine of us here, sitting in a semi-circle. It really does feel like being on top of the world. We made the 45 minute drive up from Ashland, Oregon, where I live, leaving at about 7PM, bringing along our folding chairs, layers of clothing, blankets, thermoses of hot tea, and assorted snacks. Late summer nights can get quite cold up on the mountain, even though the days can be warm and delightful.

My friend and mentor in this group, whom I will call Jennifer, has had numerous experiences with extraterrestrials, who are invisible to most of us. She is clairvoyant and sees other beings and energies quite naturally, far more than I do, and she studied with Dr. Steven Greer in the past.

I have been enamored of her fascinating stories about her interactions with ETs for several years and am excited to participate in this adventure. I have come here three other times this summer with Jennifer and this group in order to connect with star beings. We have had some sweet experiences, individually and as a group. But this night is special.

Dr. Steven M. Greer directs Sirius Disclosure, a research project working to disclose the facts about UFOs, extraterrestrial intelligence, and classified advanced energy and propulsion systems.

He and his team have interviewed more than 400 government, military, and intelligence community witnesses who have testified to their personal, first hand experience with UFOs, ETs, ET technology, and the cover-up that keeps this information secret. They strive to develop a peaceful relationship with Extraterrestrial Intelligence (ETI). **www.siriusdisclosure.com**

We are not the only ones interested in extraterrestrials. SETI, Search for Extraterrestrial Intelligence, Institute in Mountain View, California often works in association with NASA and has an observatory on the University of California, Berkeley campus. Re-

search and education based, their highly qualified scientists seek evidence of life in the universe by looking for some signature of its technology.

Before these excursions with Jennifer, I had not had much experience with ETs and I was very excited about the possibility of connecting with them. I got quite frustrated at first because it seemed that others were seeing space ships in the sky, which I didn't see.

During our previous visit, a few weeks earlier, after we had taken time to get quiet and go inward, Jennifer said that a ship had landed near us. I did not see anything but I could feel a loving presence. Under Jennifer's guidance, and in our minds' eyes, we walked to the ship and got on board. I could feel a great deal of energy. In fact, I became queasy from so much energy pulsing through me. I sensed beings all around me, telling me to lie down and rest as they worked on me. I felt myself relax and get very quiet.

Then I noticed something totally unexpected and amazing. The ship was a living, conscious being. It was almost like a whale—a huge empty, open vessel, with full consciousness—moving subtly, flowing and shifting constantly, though it was not moving physically. How wonderful! I had no idea that space ships could be alive in this way.

Even with this incredible encounter, I doubted myself. I thought I must be making it all up. But then, the next day, I had a very strong, clear message from my inner guidance. My Soul, along with Guides and Angels, said,

"You have allowed yourself to get discouraged because you don't always see, feel, or hear the entities who come to you. You feel like you are not 'tuned in' because of this. It is not so. What you are learning now, dearest one, is to tune into subtle realms that you have not experienced before. So it feels like you are not connected, but the truth is that the messages and feelings are more subtle now and you have not yet adjusted to this way of receiving information. That is part of your process: to sense on more subtle levels. It is time to start trusting whatever you see, feel, or know. By trusting you allow more in."

Because I had received this message a few weeks earlier, I am more open and trusting of whatever I might experience as I sit on the mountain on this clear September night. It feels good to just relax with it all.

When the sun sets, it gets cold quickly so we are now all bundled up in jackets and blankets, sipping hot tea from our thermoses to keep warm. The coziness of this circle and the silence of the night add to my excitement and create a beautiful setting for the connection we seek. The moon is almost full and shines brightly, peeking out from behind a huge evergreen tree.

At first, we simply sit and gaze at the obsidian night sky, which is filled with seemingly millions of sparkling stars. Flashing lights move through the heavens but these are airplanes, nothing out of the ordinary. According to Jennifer and others who have had contact with extraterrestrial beings, space ships do not blink as planes do. Actually I don't see anything that is not easily explainable and fairly commonplace. After about 20 minutes of gazing at the night sky, Jennifer guides us to turn our attention inward, each of us taking turns to speak out loud about what we feel and see with our inner awareness.

She begins by saying, "The ETs are setting up some kind of structure in front of us." Other people then start to sense something as well and seem to get bits and pieces about this etheric structure.

Suddenly, I am bursting with excitement because I can "see" it myself. Usually I don't "see" things. I more often sense them emotionally or through thoughts and words, but this I see, not with my physical eyes but with my inner vision. I say to the others, "It looks like a 3-dimensional Star of David."

How incredible is this? Today is the holiest of Jewish days, Yom Kippur, and the Star of David, often referred to as the Jewish Star, is the most sacred of Jewish symbols. It is a six-pointed star with two triangles superimposed on one another, one facing up and the other down. The Star of David is two-dimensional but what I see now is three-dimensional and alive.

I sense that the top half of it is rotating in one direction and the bottom half in the opposite direction. It seems to be taking the polarities—heaven and earth, light and dark, past and future—and somehow melding them into a singular energy. It is facilitating a glimpse into other realms, by connecting Earth and other dimensions of reality.

I learned later that night, after going home and researching it on the internet, that this form is often called a Merkaba, or Merkabah, a sacred geometric form used to transport consciousness to other realms. I was truly amazed to learn that the structure I had seen, the three-dimensional Star of David with counter-rotating fields of energy, was exactly what was described as a Merkaba by some sources. I found an illustration that beautifully illustrated all aspects of this sacred geometric form that I had experienced.

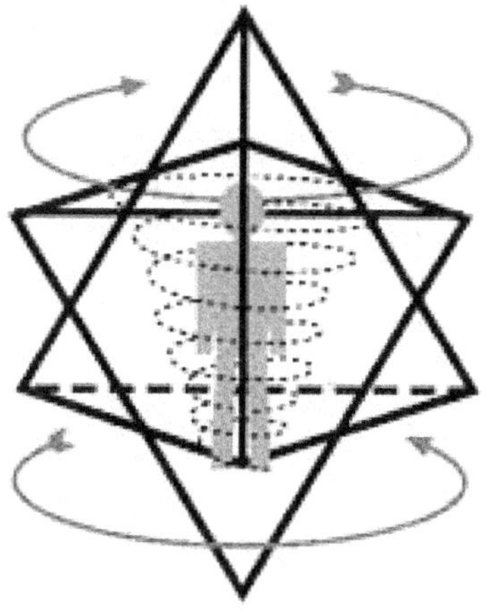

I read online that in ancient Egyptian texts, "the word Merkaba is actually comprised of three separate words: Mer, which means light, Ka, which means spirit, and Ba, which means body. Put together, these three words connote the union of spirit and body, surrounded by light. The symbol, which takes the shape of a star, is believed to be a divine vehicle made entirely of light and designed to transport or connect the spirit and body to higher realms."

As I read further that night, I learned that some modern esoteric teachings say that the Merkaba consists of two equally sized, interlocked tetrahedra of light with a common center, where one tetrahedron, or triangular pyramid, points up and the other down. In his books, renowned researcher and physicist Drunvalo Melchizedek describes the Merkaba as a "Star Tetrahedron," since it can be viewed as a three-dimensional Star of David.

Drunvalo has said that the Merkaba is an ancient vehicle of ascension, acknowledged by Hebrews and Egyptians alike. Ascension is a process where the human body is transformed into light and birthed into a new world that transcends the human limitations of this reality. In ancient Hebrew, the word merkaba, or mercava, translates as chariot, so it was also seen as a vehicle facilitating travel to other realms.

Credo Mutwa, now deceased spiritual leader of the Zulu tribe in Africa, told Drunvalo that Merkaba is also a Zulu word meaning a space/time/dimension vehicle. According to Zulu legend, his entire tribe had come from another dimension to Earth using the Merkaba.

It surprised me to learn that this word, merkaba, is recognized in several different countries and languages, in Egypt, Israel, and South Africa. To me, this means that it is an ancient, sacred symbol that has been with human beings for a long, long time. I felt so privileged to have been given a glimpse of this incredible ascension vehicle.

However, in this moment, sitting on the mountain in the stillness of a September night and sensing this 3-D Star of David, on the holy day of Yom Kippur, I don't know any of this. I only know what I see and feel. It is our group's common intent and serious focus that seems to have facilitated the presence of this Merkaba, a gift from the higher beings who now surround us. I can't see these beings, but I do sense their presence. It feels like sitting in the lap of a wise, nurturing, beloved grandmother.

Suddenly, seemingly out of nowhere, I sense the presence of Elephants. I know this feeling well. After all, I have communicated with them for years and have written a book about them, so I know what their group consciousness feels like. But what the heck are elephants doing on a mountain in southern Oregon?

I receive a message that touches me to my core and resonates within me as profound truth. What I hear is that I carry the Elephants with me energetically because we are so deeply connected. I had brought them here for the higher beings to work with them. This structure, the Merkaba, is working with the Elephants and helping them do their own work as well as allowing us a doorway to see into other dimensions.

I then see, with my inner vision, a semi-circle of Elephants filling the heavens with their big bodies, brilliant light emanating from each one. These are Elephants who have died on Earth and are now in spirit form, light beings without physical bodies. Many, many Elephants on Earth have died recently, mostly from poaching for the ivory of their tusks. They have often suffered painful deaths and I have been deeply troubled by what is happening, as have so many other people.

These Elephants in my vision, however, are light-filled, loving, and happy. They are connected intimately, spiritually, with Elephants embodied on Earth, who form the lower half of the circle that I am witnessing. So there is a huge circle of Elephants, those in Spirit above and those embodied on Earth below.

By connecting energetically this way, the Elephants' intention of grounding, stabilization, and harmony for this planet is vastly amplified.

Wow! I am in heaven, so to speak. Bliss hardly describes the feeling of love and joy coming through this extraordinary scene. I know that the Elephants who have died are flooding Earth with light and healing, not just for Elephants but for all life on Earth.

Even though I have felt deep grief at their plight, now I know that these beings, once out of their physical bodies, are not suffering. Quite the contrary. They are radiating energy to the Elephants who are still in form and are creating a huge bubble of healing light around the planet. The image fades and I am left sitting, awestruck, in my chair.

I excitedly share my vision with the others in our group and they feel the joy of it as well. In fact, we are all giddy after this and a few of us do the "elephant stomp." We get up from our chairs and dance around, some of us putting our arms together and swinging them back and forth like elephant trunks while making trumpeting sounds. Elephant magic has come to life in all of us.

It is getting late and our time on the mountain is coming to an end. We pack up all our gear to drive home in our cars. As I sit in *the passenger seat in one of these vehicles, I still feel energized and a little dizzy, my mind swirling with wonder and gratitude for what I have received. Now I know that the Elephants who die at the hands of humans do not die in vain. Although their bodies die, their spirit lives on and serves other Elephants and the Earth herself. What a precious gift they offer.*

REFLECTIONS ON ELEPHANTS IN THE SKY

While writing about my experience of seeing Elephants in the sky several years after it happened, I realized how hard it is to describe a mystical experience like this in words. If I had read someone else's rendition of it, I might have thought that the writer had a very strong imagination and something like this is simply not possible.

But I know what I experienced and I can still feel it. The vision of light-filled Elephants radiating that light to Earth has come to me many, many times since that night, and has changed my inner reality. It gives me an enormous sense of relief and fascination. Knowing there is a bigger picture, that these Elephants who have died can find peace, light, love, and joy when released from their physical bodies and then share that with their beloved earthbound relatives, gives me a sense of hope and awe. Who am I to judge why things happen as they do? That is the work of a power far greater than what I can comprehend, and I can only marvel at the mystery.

I have held this image in my heart for years; it helps me see that even in the face of horrendous and inexcusable acts of violence, there can be a positive outcome on the other side of the veil. That gives me comfort. At the same time, I am ever more saddened and angry at the heinous destruction humankind has wrought on this planet, including the needless abuse and killing of elephants and many other species. I know this reality weighs heavily on many people, especially those of us who love animals and the natural world so deeply. We cannot help but be impacted.

However, this powerful vision gives me hope, as well as faith in a much greater reality. May it do the same for you.

CHAPTER 16

ELEPHANTS ON THE GROUND

You have told me over and over again that, just as I saw in the vision of Elephants in the Sky, the way to survive the devastation that is occurring on Earth at this time is to see everything from a higher spiritual perspective and not get caught up in the drama that is continually playing out in our physical reality. Not to live in denial of what is going on, but to anchor ourselves in a much higher vibration than the very low vibration of hatred and violence. When we can come from love, light, hope, and peace, we raise the consciousness of everyone and everything we touch. And that, along with positive action from a loving heart, will change the course of history. Anger and violence only create more of the same.

Although I know this is true, I still feel deeply disturbed by what is happening to elephants now on this planet. The amazing vision of Elephants of light that I had on the mountain gave me hope and inspiration. But even so, I still grieve when an animal dies. Or when a human being dies for that matter. Can you help me with this? How do you deal with it? How can I put it into perspective and not get so deeply upset when I hear of a brutal killing?

As long as you live on this Earth, you will suffer emotionally when something happens that hurts your heart. It is part of the earthly experience and it cannot be changed unless you decide to close your heart entirely and live without compassion.

You have consciously chosen to be more compassionate, not less. And with this compassion comes pain. But it also brings great joy. When something loving and positive happens to yourself or another, you feel happy. But you cannot have great happiness without the pain, or vice versa. It is all about an open heart and allowing yourself to feel.

So many people these days have shut down emotionally and don't let themselves feel. It is just too painful and they cannot cope. They have become the living dead.

Do not think something is wrong when you grieve the loss of something precious. There is a deep connection you feel with physical reality, with physical bodies. The loss of someone can be painful, especially if that death comes with violence and abuse. And, in truth, this is what can lead to positive action.

How does grief lead to positive action?

Grief opens the heart and can lead to righteous anger, which is a much more conscious form of anger. This is different from the anger that leads to senseless violence. Righteous or holy anger creates a sense of passion about making changes so the tragedy that was experienced can't occur again. The action that can result from directing that anger can be powerful and life-changing.

You, no doubt, have witnessed this many times when a person has gone through a devastating experience and then has become a passionate and dedicated agent for change. Conscious anger can lead to sacred action.

We too, as elephants in bodies, suffer the pain of loss. Just because we can transcend pain to a certain degree does not mean we do not experience pain and grief at all. We certainly do. We are all—humans, elephants, and many others—learning to balance body and soul, physical and nonphysical, Earth and other dimensions. It is part of what we do here, on this planet.

Please be gentle with yourself. This is not an easy lesson, or an easy planet to live upon. But we are all here together, and together we can overcome great travails. Let us love and work together for the betterment of all.

Thank you so much. This helps, but I had thought that with this higher vision I would be better able to cope with individuals dying and the dying of species. However, I still grieve deeply. Is there a way to ease this process and go to higher realms, not getting so caught up in the drama?

How do you, or we, accept these deaths without losing our balance and peace of mind? How do we embody the Divine while living in body on Earth? That is the real question, isn't it?

We are not experts on this topic. We can only speak from our own experience. When one of us dies, we do grieve deeply and we honor that one. We honor him or her by remembering them in a positive light, by touching the body when we can, and allowing ourselves to feel the loss. There is definitely a missing space in our hearts and minds when one of us dies and it takes time to fill that hole.

How do we fill it? By holding that Elephant within our loving awareness and realizing that the space they occupied in our hearts will always be there and no one can ever replace them. They are with us forever. Over time, the sadness lessens and may disappear. But their presence is always with us.

Beautiful, but what about babies that don't have this level of awareness? I know they can suffer deeply after the loss of their mothers, just as human babies do. When I spent time at Sheldrick Wildlife Trust in Kenya, the most successful orphan-elephant rescue and rehabilitation program in the world, I learned that babies can easily die of grief when they have lost their mothers.

At the orphanage, caretakers are with the babies 24/7. They rotate caretakers because babies can become too attached and dependent on one person and then again suffer a deep sense of abandonment if that person is not present. So they are careful to avoid this by having more than one person work with each baby.

Babies do not cope as easily. A baby who has lost her mother may never recover. We do our best to help heal their grief, but it is not always enough. They don't have the maturity and experience to go on and may die of grief. That is simply how it is and we have to live with that reality.

People who nourish and aid young ones who cannot cope on their own are a great blessing for us. It is sacred, holy work and we are deeply grateful.

As adult Elephants, we know that life goes on and the soul does not die. Young ones are not able to hold both realities, but the elders have learned to do this, and so there is great comfort in knowing that the one who left us physically is not gone spiritually, energetically. This helps a great deal.

Are you able to sense the one who has died? All those Elephants of light that I saw in the sky were so happy and loving. Can you sense them too?

Only with our inner awareness. As we said, babies don't yet have that capacity. They are too immersed in grief. And adults who are in deep grief cannot either. But once the grief passes, we are, for the most part, able to traverse both worlds: physical life on Earth and the spiritual life that transcends earthly awareness. Like you, we are not attuned to other dimensions all the time. But we can move into these realms at times, and we do. More so when we are at peace—which is becoming more rare as our lives are disrupted by things outside of our control or desire.

You have told me that you can transcend earthly reality when you are in pain. So I would assume this means you can move to higher dimensions at will. Is this not so?

It is so to a degree. We can let go of this reality more readily than most humans can because we are not as attached to our mental process. However, when there is great emotion, especially negative emotion, it is far more difficult to do this. When we are calm, at peace, content, it is fairly easy. When we are upset in any way—scared, sad, angry—it is not as easy. It is becoming more challenging as our habitat is lost and as more and more elephants are killed. We are often on high alert.

I am so sorry for the unconsciousness, insensitivity, greed, and ignorance of so many humans. I wish I could change it, but I cannot. Often I am ashamed to be part of this species that is so destructive. I can only apologize and ask forgiveness. I don't know what else to do.

Dear friend, as we have told you many, many times in the past, there is nothing for you to apologize for. There is nothing to forgive. All is in divine order and we accept this, probably far more than you do. Yes, we get angry. Yes, we grieve. Yes, we lose control and lose ourselves at times. But overall, we just go on. We don't try to sort it out and understand everything as you do. We simply live. Do not take on this responsibility. It is not yours. It is only yours to love us and love your-self and others. Not to suffer because of the unconscious actions of others. By being a conscious, loving person you can share your love and awareness of our situation with others and, in that way, help us immensely.

Thank you for caring so deeply. Not an easy path, but it is what will, in the end, save us all from hatred, war, and violence on this dear and beloved planet.

ACTION

I so appreciate your beautiful words, but you have not addressed the need for physical action on this planet in order to end the violence and to help save elephants and other species, including ourselves. Spiritual action is not enough. So can you please talk about this?

You are right. Spiritual action is not enough. And perhaps we have focused on this too much and not enough on what is happening here and now on planet Earth, and what humans can do to stop it.

Some things are unstoppable, such as the Earth's own evolutionary process. But human caused pollution and destruction can certainly be quelled by conscious action. This can take many forms, but the only effective action is undertaken by loving attention to the guidance of the Divine. We, as physical beings living on Earth, are so limited in our capacities. But our souls know all. When someone acts from an open heart and embodied soul, everything is possible. So our best advice to you and other human beings who truly want to help us, and to make a positive impact on this planet, is to open your hearts, listen to the callings of your soul, and be prepared to act according to that divine inner guidance.

CHAPTER 17

TWO SISTERS

I call now for the two Sister Elephants that I am sensing. Can you tell me why you are with me now?

We came to you because, although it is wonderful and informative to communicate with group consciousness, there is also value in speaking with certain individuals.

As you have seen in your work with companion animals, there is great power in reaching the individual soul. And so it is with the wild ones. It is not necessary to know an individual in the physical plane in order to communicate with that being. Sometimes it is helpful, and other times it distracts.

Because you do not know us in the physical realm, we can say what we choose to say and you are able to hear it, without having to bypass your conscious mind. The conscious mind contains images and ideas based on past history and exposure. Sometimes these images get in the way and form a sort of box where anything outside the box is too foreign to let in. So, because we have not met you in physical form, we have an advantage; no preconceived ideas, and certainly no expectations.

We come to you in love, peace, and gratitude. We have much to say if you care to listen.

Who are you?

We are Elephants without bodies. We have lived before. And when we passed on into another dimension, we took our Elephant consciousness with us. We are, indeed, two sisters. Sister Elephants, Sister Souls, and sisters to you, in a spiritual sense.

We come to you now for one great reason: to teach you what we represent, not only as elephants on the physical plane, but as spirits in another reality. You see, dear friend, there are many planes of reality and many dimensions. Each carries its own vibration. As you see an elephant on the earthly plane, embodying certain characteristics, so these characteristics have a different meaning at other levels of existence.

For instance, the Elephants spoke to you about our trunks and you were invited to explore the great value of trunks in physical reality. At the same time, the trunk carries over into different realms, not as a physical structure, but as an energetic configuration. After we cross over to the spirit world through physical death, the trunk carries our energy and distributes it. Just as we can spray water or dirt with our trunks to cleanse our bodies, we can use our spiritual trunks to spread wisdom, love, and beauty in other dimensions.

Our huge feet make an enormous impact on the Earth—like big drums as we walk. The pounding of the earth beneath our feet sends vibrations within, on, and under the ground, which is then perceived by other elephants. Sometimes this pounding, or drumming, serves as a wake up call. At other times, it is a mechanism to alter consciousness, just as drums are often used by humans.

When we transcend earthly reality, our feet are used in a similar way. Of course, we do not walk on the ground because we are not present in physical bodies any longer. But our feet are still energetically able to produce a vibration similar to that of drumming.

What then is the purpose of these vibrations, once you are no longer embodied in physical form?

Just as on Earth, as our footfalls relay messages through the ground, so, in the spirit realm, the feet serve a similar function. They are a means of communication.

I thought that when you no longer have a body, you can communicate with others in a flash of thought and intention. So why would this be necessary?

Of course, we don't need bodies in order to relate to other beings once we are in the Spirit realm. So it would make sense that sending messages through foot vibrations would be unnecessary. But there is another aspect to this that you have not considered.

When we say that our feet transmit energy, it is not so different from what we spoke about with our trunks. We shower others with light and love through our trunks. Of course now we are speaking about a plane of existence, perhaps what you call the astral, that precedes the loss of our bodies altogether. So when you talk about connecting with another being in a flash of inspiration, this holds true on higher planes. But when we speak of the energetic body, we are talking about a level of existence not so far removed from the Earth; a transition zone. In this place, it is not as easy to simply show up somewhere else by using thought and intention. Therefore, if we want to connect or communicate with another elephant, or a different kind of being, it is easy to send those vibrations through our feet. We are used to it, having done it regularly when we were embodied on Earth.

You said that the feet in etheric elephants are used to communicate. But on Earth, the feet stomp the ground and then the vibrations travel through a substrate, the ground. I see it as molecules bombarding one another, thus sending a signal. Or when you vocalize sounds, these travel through the air. So there is always a substrate that gets impacted. When you die, there is no substrate, as I understand it. Your feet can't make noise or vibrations on their own. They need to touch something. So how can this work?

When you say there is no substrate in the etheric realm, it is the same as saying that we don't have bodies at all. There is substance. It is simply not as defined or dense as it is on Earth. Almost translucent.

There are all manner of things in this realm, but they are much lighter and may perform a slightly different function than they did in purely physical form. The colors may be brighter because they are light-filled.

So when we say we use our trunks to disperse light and our feet to send energetic communication, it is because in this realm—an in-between space, between physical and non-physical realities—we send out these vibrations energetically. There is ground to stand upon. It is just not as dense as on Earth. Now does it make more sense?

Yes. It is just hard for me to imagine this being true. But I believe you and so I trust that it is real.

Where do you think you go in your dreams?

I am not sure. An imaginal realm? Other dimensions?

So it is. Another dimension. This is what we describe. When you leave your body, you move into another dimension, a completely different reality. It is a preparation ground for the next step, which is loss of the body altogether.

What is it like when you lose the body completely?

You will remember your vision of Elephants as light in the sky. They represent the next stage of development: when we lose our physical and etheric bodies and become light. This is what you saw. And because of this experience, you were elevated to a whole new level of consciousness. That is why that experience was so critically important for you and why it has stuck with you so intensely.

Yes, that was a powerful experience for me. Is there anything more you want to say about what it is like when you are light beings and have shed the etheric body?

Yes. When we shed the body, physically and then energetically, we move into another dimension where all is made of light and love. There are no physical bodies or impediments to distract us or detain us from what we need to be. In this plane of existence we have a mission, and that is to evolve Humanity and planet Earth.

This must only apply to those beings connected with Earth. Do others work with different planets and star systems?

Yes, of course. We came here intentionally to help planet Earth evolve in consciousness, which means primarily assisting humans in their evolution.

Where did you come from?

We came from another star system far away from here many years ago, when the Earth was being formed. As Earth evolved, so did our physical form. We are now in the latest version, but this does not mean it is the last.

Are you saying that you will continue to evolve spiritually as well as physically, and that your form will be different over time?

Yes, as will yours. You are not the final incarnation of humans. That is unless you choose, as a species, to destroy your own habitat on Earth. There is great potential for further evolution.

Are you assisting with this process?

Yes. We hold that intention for Humanity and for all life forms on this planet. We cannot do it for you, but we can certainly contribute to the energy that will inspire this to take place.

Is there anything else you want to say about this?

We want you to know that there are many other realms and dimensions. Planet Earth, in her physical form, is only one. Open your mind to possibilities and you may be awed by the immense variety of life forms and the expansiveness that exists.

SISTERS IN SPIRIT

Tell me, Sisters, do you have names?

Your human names are not appropriate for who we are. Here, in Spirit, it is only our presence that identifies us. We are so present with one another that nothing else is necessary or required. For the purposes of your writing, we will identify ourselves as The Sisters. This is enough.

Thank you. Can you help me understand the concepts you described earlier a little better?

Yes. The idea is that after physical death, the body energetically lives on in spirit form. And each structure still has a function, although it is slightly different from the function it served on Earth. In other words, the organ or structure serves a purpose metaphorically or symbolically similar to the function served by the physical body. It is much like consciousness. On Earth, your consciousness is set up to relate to things on a physical level. You are able to tap into higher realms, but for the sake of survival, you need to maneuver in a physical world.

When your body dies and is no longer necessary, you, your consciousness, moves into the realm of Spirit. Whatever you learned in physical form, you take with you. You don't need to use this awareness any more to survive in a physical reality, so the awareness becomes a way of maneuvering in a bodiless form.

I am feeling a little uncomfortable expressing these ideas. I have not studied religion or philosophy enough to know about these concepts.

And what makes you think that teachers and philosophers have all the answers? It is because you are so open to new ideas that this information comes to you. Do you really think that anyone truly knows what happens after death? Do you think that anyone really knows how we, as animals, operate on this physical plane or in other dimensions? Why would anyone have more insight and understanding than you do, as an interested, curious, open-minded, evolved soul who has dedicated her life to this work?

That helps a lot. I think of spiritual teachers as far more enlightened, aware, and knowledgeable than I am. People who have studied spirituality and lived it their entire lives certainly have a higher perspective. Don't they?

Not necessarily. How many spiritual teachers say that animals do not have individual souls? Clearly they are coming from a different perspective than you are. And so, in this case, you have an advantage. You are not limited by teachings of others or previous beliefs.

Another example of this is the idea that animals have sometimes been humans in other lifetimes, and vice versa. Many spiritual teachers do not believe this is possible. But for you, this awareness has come through your own experience and openness. It may seem far out to some, but this is your reality. In the end, it is all you can truly trust.

RELATIONSHIPS

Can you speak about relationships and social structure in Elephants on Earth? It is a topic of interest to me now. I want deeper relationships and would like to learn about this from you.

In our elephant world, there are two levels to our relationships: that of the physical world and that of the spiritual. Sometimes the two do not meet, but when they do, it is a blessing. All flows well and we are joyful. When we are distracted by anger, frustration, and all the base emotions, we may lose touch with our spiritual selves, and then chaos ensues. But when we align with Spirit and our own highest and deepest natures, our lives are heavenly.

In our physical world, when we function well as a group, we experience harmony and love. The matriarch leads us, and we are willing to follow, for the most part. Sometimes there are conflicts, but usually we are pretty calm about the situation. We know that when we have a clear leader, everything flows more smoothly. If it happens that the matriarch is not in alignment with the group, we will challenge her and depose her. But this rarely happens. Usually there is agreement about who will lead us. We know one another well enough to make those choices wisely.

Just as in human families, each elephant is an individual with a personality. Sometimes it is challenging to put up with one another, and there are arguments and disagreements. Occasionally we fight it out. But usually we resolve our issues more gently. When we are connected to Spirit, grounded in our beingness rather than solely in our personalities, we can communicate in subtle ways and resolve most conflicts. We come to agreement in this way, and then our lives are peaceful and flow smoothly.

From this place, we honor one another's differences, and we revel in our similarities. There is little to squabble about, and so we don't. Similarly, if people could live this way, aligned with their higher natures, much conflict would never occur. Most things could be resolved spiritually.

When we are living in this place of harmony, we move almost as one body. Our movements are slow and easy. We don't worry about things. We enjoy our lives and our community. It is a peaceful way of living.

I can feel it. I sense the relaxation you describe. It is wonderful. But what about when things do not work so smoothly? What do you do?

If there is a disruption in our world, we may lose our sense of equilibrium and inner peace. It is as if we lose the sense of self and community that sustains us. These are the times when we get into trouble with people, and we seem destructive and angry. Our emotions take over and interfere with our spiritual connection to our highest selves.

Our job as matriarchs, as leaders, is to help pull the herd back into balance. We try our best to maintain our sense of connectedness with our spiritual natures. When we remain in this place of love and peace, we can influence the other animals to get back to this calm and deliberate state of being. We project that sense of peace onto others and they receive it, unless the disruption has simply been too intense. Then we need to wait until order is somehow restored, either from outside or from a wellspring contained within us.

Our lives are not so different from the lives of humans. What we do have, that perhaps many of you do not, is the cohesion of the group and the resources available to us through our divine connection with our own true natures. This is available to you as well, and we encourage you to continue to pursue and maintain the highest relationship with your Divine Spirit.

The information I received from the Matriarchs is that elephants choose the matriarch, but what I have heard from human researchers who have studied elephants for years is that the oldest female elephant becomes the matriarch. Can you speak to me about this?

There is a higher principle at work here that may not be apparent to most humans; an internal structure within our elephant society that works for us. A matriarch is born to be matriarch. Not solely because she is an elder or according to any rule or concept. It is part of her nature. And when it is time to lead, she steps forward.

Of course, experience is a wise teacher, so it usually turns out that the matriarch is one of the oldest in the herd, if not the oldest. She also has been trained by those preceding her in the ways of leadership. But, in a sense, it is preordained. She simple steps into her role, her position, with dignity and grace.

Occasionally, others in the herd do not agree and may challenge her. But this is rare. When it does occur, the rest of the herd steps in and decides what to do.

INDIVIDUALITY

Dear Sisters, I do not sense your individual personalities. Actually, to me you don't feel much different from the energy I feel in communicating with Elephants in general. Can you please explain this?

In the traditional sense, if you think of us as sisters, you will get bogged down. In Spirit, we are not personalities or individuals in the same way you are on Earth. Our energies meld and blend, and so it is very difficult to differentiate one from another.

But I have worked with individual animal souls many times. This is what I do when I connect with a companion animal or even a wild animal's soul. What is that about?

Beings retain their individuality for some time after they transition out of their bodies. As we evolve in spirit and lose touch more and more with our physical bodies, we become lighter and less attached to physical reality. And then our personalities melt away. We have our uniqueness intact to some degree, but it is not so obvious any longer.

It seems, though, that I can contact the individual souls of beings who have lived many years ago. How do you explain this?

The consciousness is always there. It never disappears, but after a while, most beings move into Oneness and no longer identify with their individuated selves. This, however, is always available to them and to you, but mostly they choose not to inhabit this separate reality any longer, unless there is a specific reason to call it in.

Is it true that you are Sisters in Spirit?

Yes. And also part of the greater Elephant consciousness. For this reason, it is hard for you to separate out. But it really doesn't matter. The information is the same. This way, though, we can be with you more individually and personally. As guiding spirits if you like.

I do like it. The more help and support I can get the better!

CHAPTER 18

ELEPHANT WISDOM

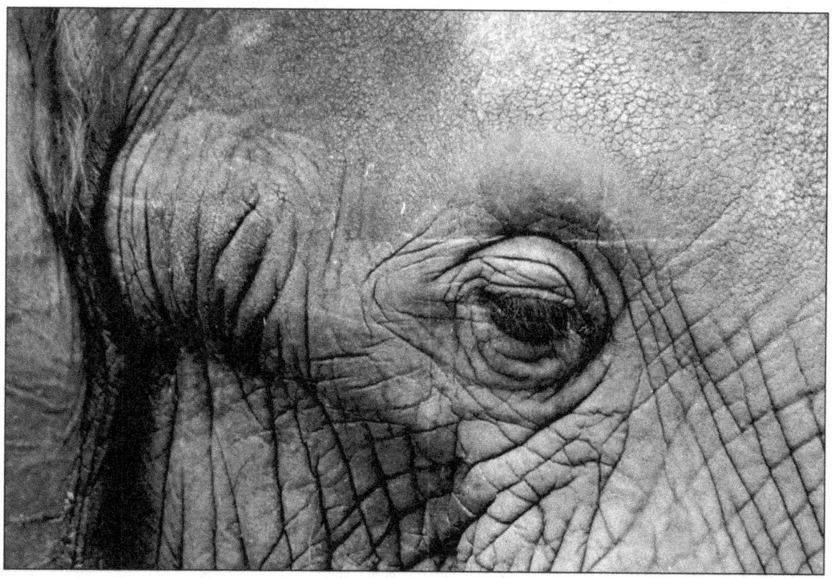

My dear Elephant friends, I have loved you for many years. To me, you represent grounding, stability, compassion, strength, courage, and wisdom. Is there anything you want to say about these qualities and who you really are, as souls and as physical beings?

As we embody these wonderful traits, we also embody other traits that are not as beautiful to you. For example, we have enormous tempers. We often get angry and can inflict damage, due to our great size and strength.

If you see us from a spiritual perspective, you see the beautiful qualities of strength, courage, and wisdom; but, on this earthly plane, our shadow side is also evident. We remind you that all physical beings embody negative as well as positive qualities. It is all part of the whole. To love one side you must love and embrace the other. Until you accept the dark you will never be fully in the light.

One of the lessons of this planet is to live with polarity. Until you accept and embrace the shadow within yourself, you will never be whole. There is great peace that comes with total acceptance. We ask you to consider this and apply it to your daily life.

You speak of accepting negative traits, which I understand. However, negative traits can be taken too far. There is much violence, prejudice, greed, and hatred in the human world. Not all of this negativity can be accepted or condoned. It must be changed.

We agree. Even in our own society there is too much violence. We have mentioned musth in bulls, when testosterone levels are high; a very intense time for us. Yet, we know it serves a purpose. We are highly emotional beings and we need an outlet.

We know from our own experience that people are often violent, greedy, and cruel. This is not acceptable behavior, and so we arrive at a dichotomy: how do you accept the shadow and, at the same time, learn to control it?

You must learn to be with these bothersome emotions, accept them as they are, and release them as necessary. For instance, we speak of anger, the cause of much violence. The anger is present. If you try to ignore it, it will only increase in intensity.

Allow yourself to feel it. Then there are choices: take this anger out on others and harm them; turn the anger inward and harm yourself; or redirect the anger into something harmful to no one. There are many outlets: physical activity such as dance or sports, mental activity, creative expression, spiritual, emotional, or psychological work, or simply being aggressive with inanimate objects. Ultimately, the energy behind the anger may be used as a force for good. The key is recognizing, accepting, and expressing the emotion.

MEMORY

It has been said that elephants have incredible memories. Can you please speak about this?

We have good memories, and, in physical form, we are quite intelligent. People who know us and work with us know we are not "dumb animals." Actually, we are not so different from other animals; we do not want animals to be judged by their intelligence, memory, or any other physical quality. A bee is as valuable and worthy of love as we are, even though it does not necessarily respond in a way humans understand or relate to.

We are blessed with great memories. We can remember happenings, places, and others we have encountered along the way. We remember things of the cosmos and carry the wisdom of other realms and realities. We bring this wisdom to planet Earth. As do the Whales.

Perhaps you think it necessary to describe this in great detail, but it is not what is most important. Instead, we would like this book to be about our relationship with the Earth and with Humanity; how we can make our home a better place in which to live. That is our primary focus in these communications.

SELF-DOUBT

I constantly struggle with self-doubt. Do you have any insights or suggestions to help me?

You, like all who live on this planet, were created from matter and Spirit[7]. Although we were created from something tangible and substantial, we are nothing without the Spirit that sustains our life force.

On Earth, the body is the container in which Spirit inhabits. In other words, your Spirit is infinite, and your body is finite. Because of this, there is polarity, duality, or contrast, and with this duality also comes self-doubt.

Why? As we see it, humans have infinite choice and possibility. We, as animals, do not. The soul, of course, always has free choice, but as physical beings, we are somewhat limited. This is because we are locked into forms which are limited by our capabilities. We must

---

7   I capitalize Spirit because I see it as a realm, or energy unto itself. I capitalize Earth for the same reason. One definition of spirit is: the vital principle in humans, animating the body or mediating between body and soul. Others use it as synonymous with the soul. To me, the Soul lives within the spiritual realm, or within Spirit. I refer to human or animal Spirit as the manifestation of the Soul that inhabits the body. The Soul, for me, is that ineffable essence of our true nature. It is that part of us that inhabits the Spirit realm and is without form, directly associated with the Divine. It is the Divine within us.

inhabit certain areas and live particular lifestyles in order to survive. Humans are different.

Because of their capacity to create what they need and want, humans are not limited by the climate or habitat in which they can naturally survive. They can create what they need anywhere. But, because they have the power to create, they also have the power to destroy. It is inherent in the nature of duality.

What does this have to do with self-doubt?

Because of this capacity to create and destroy on a large scale, there is great power that resides within each human being. Having this capacity is a tremendous responsibility. With that responsibility often comes fear. One can create great things but can also wreak great destruction. Because this power is so awesome, through millennia people have learned to fear it. This fear is reinforced by the domination and destruction they have witnessed. This translates into fear of self and eventually to self-hatred and self-doubt.

This makes sense. Being a woman in my culture has an effect as well. Women have been dominated by men for a long time; it is ingrained in many of us to doubt ourselves. I want to get over it! Do you have any advice?

We do have some suggestions, but it is up to you to resolve this for yourself. We can only support and encourage you. What we see in you and many of your kind is a tendency to think that the work you do is unimportant, that your life is not as good as it could be, that you are not enough as you are. You find ways to sabotage yourself and then feel angry and dejected. It is a vicious cycle that occurs in many humans, particularly in your culture where there is a strong attachment to accomplishment. When you don't accomplish great things, and even when you do, there is always more and better you could be doing.

We encourage you to focus solely on what is good and positive in your life, the accomplishments you have already achieved, and the great blessings you have been given.

You and others who have been conditioned from childhood in this manner often focus on what you don't have and what is wrong rather than what is good and right. By living with this reality, you create more of it; a sense of lack and insufficiency, a constant state of frustration and anxiety.

Dearest one, we love you and we know who you are. If you and others could see yourselves through our eyes, you would not question yourself ever again. We offer you the knowing that you are deeply cherished by Spirit, by all the beings inhabiting the unseen world, and that each and every thing you do or say is just as it needs to be. Mistakes are inevitable and are great teachers. Learn from them rather than beating yourself up for making them. Find the blessing in each moment and live from appreciation rather than criticism. In this way, you grow to love and honor yourself as well as everything and everyone else you encounter.

FREE CHOICE

Is it true that the Soul always has free choice?

Yes. But we will explain. The soul of animals is not so different from the soul of humans, as we are all made from the same substance. In the Spirit realm, where there are no bodies, and limitations do not apply as on Earth, the soul has free reign. The soul can move from place to place, thought to thought, realm to realm, in a flash of awareness and intent. It is up to the individual soul whether or not to individuate or to be in a group, or whether to be conscious or not when embodied. All choices are available and accessible. This holds true for all souls.

Does this answer your question?

Yes, thank you. Is there more you would like to say on this matter?

Yes. Men and women have the power of choice and the responsibility those choices entail. The animals are under human dominion or domination—however that may be perceived. It is not our conscious choice to be captives. It is not our choice to have our lands destroyed and taken over. It is not our choice to be used and abused by humans.

It is, however, our choice to be here. And in being here, we accept the consequences. We know that much of what is happening on this planet is not deliberate, and not done through conscious choice. That is the problem. Conscious decision making in alignment with the survival of Earth and all her inhabitants is rare. Most human choices are made from a place of self-serving ego needs and desires. The heart and soul are left out of the process much of the time. This is what we mean by unconscious choices.

We intend this book to help change that unconscious decision making process; to change people's thinking and ways of looking at their lives, to become more conscious in their choices and again be in alignment with the natural world.

The animals are not perfect. We have our issues as well. We are not always the benevolent beings some people idealize us to be. We do unkind things. We live by our instincts and often act on impulse. Therefore, we are not here to judge you.

What we do offer is wisdom that comes from a very deep and strong connection with our inner spiritual nature and a wellspring of knowledge and love that comes from a place far beyond the man-made world. We offer a connection with Spirit that surpasses many people's current reality.

Our teachings are basic and simple. Truth is basic and simple. Nothing so profound or complicated is said here that a genius or master needs to interpret. Truth is truth. You will feel it in your bones when it speaks to you. That is how you determine what is true, how you assess the authenticity of a thing or an idea or a word: you sense it in your body.

Once you asked us: "Why do I write this book? Why do I believe and trust that I can communicate with animals, when, after all, I am a skeptic?"

The answer: you feel it in your body. You sense it in your heart. You know it in your entire being. That is why you communicate with animals. It is why you write this book; why you cry as you write. You feel it in deep within your body, mind, and soul. Truth is truth, and you recognize it.

HIGHER CONSCIOUSNESS

Can you speak about why most human beings have difficulty accessing higher consciousness?

Yes, we are happy to. As humans, you are born into a strange and interesting situation. You have tremendous potential; the capacity to make great changes and do wondrous things. Yet you are often stuck in a paradigm that limits your self-expression. Why?

When you come into this incarnation, you begin as an utterly help-less and dependent newborn baby. With nurturing and conditioning by adults, you grow and mature into adulthood. Wouldn't it be easier if you just dropped down here to do what you are here to do, without all the "stuff" associated with learning and growing? Think about the trials and errors you experience in order to develop into adults.

Yes, it would be easier. And boring! The laughter and tears of a child make life worth living, do they not? Part of the mystery, the excitement, the wonder of life on Earth is the process of evolution. And part of the special gift to you, as humans, is the ability to freely choose what life you will lead.

Life is a game, but in this game there are no winners or losers. The prize is learning as much as you can, loving as deeply and as intimately as you can, enjoying life, and dying with dignity and grace. If you do not accomplish these things, you have another try. If you do, you go on to other things.

This makes no sense to me. You say there are no winners or losers, and yet some people are not able to love well or to find their life's true work or to die with dignity and grace. So there are losers. I don't get your point.

Okay. Let's try again. Say you are born into a family that cherishes you, teaches you to love yourself and everyone else, and supports you in all you do and who you are. The chances of finding your true work and a loving partner are greater than if you had come from a family that did not honor, respect, or support you. Right?

Yes.

Is this an example of unfairness: that those born lucky do well in life, while those who come from poverty (in any sense of the word) are destined to live lives of misery and despair?

It sure could be seen that way.

So the person who comes from hard beginnings is most likely destined to live a life of difficulty, while the person who comes from abundance is most likely to have a happy and satisfying life. Is this true?

Actually, it isn't. Many people who seem to have everything are still miserable, and many people who have nothing and had a difficult childhood grow up to be happy and do well. What does this have to do with my question?

Each person faces his or her own challenges. Each has the capacity to make choices. Most can decide what direction to take, regardless of early conditioning and nurturing experiences, or lack of. That is the great gift of being human. If it were all handed to you, there might be less emotional growth and, as a result, diminished contentment. Instead, you are each given certain personalities, experiences, and environments in which to learn and grow. The choices are up to you, and it is only through these choices that true personal and spiritual growth occur.

You have spiritual guides and teachers; many beings supporting and loving you along the way. All of you. If you were to see, hear, feel, and know these guides from the beginning, it might be too easy to relinquish responsibility for your own choices. Instead, your guides ask you to have faith in the fact that they are here.

What about those born into poverty, abuse, exploitation, disease, and other difficult situations? Many of them simply cannot escape because they don't have the means to do it. Why does this occur? And why are many people not able to sense their inner guidance and gain comfort and support when they need it?

The truth is that you, as humans, will never fully understand all the nuances of the world. This is simply part of the Mystery. However, we have insights that might rest your mind a bit.

Each being is given a life to live on Earth. Each one has a different set of experiences to encounter. This is true of all beings, human and non-human. A pine tree, an ant, or an elephant, for instance, has certain requirements that limit where it can live. These conditions are set at birth, and life moves from there. Likewise, each individual is given a body and a set of qualities that define who that one is physically. These things are set and cannot be changed.

What creates this has been debated by humans for millennia. Let's call it God, Creative Force, Great Spirit, Allah, Yahweh, or Source. The name is not important. It is a creative power.

If people were to truly know God, the light and the power would be so overwhelming it would blind the eyes and overtax the consciousness of its witness. You are simply not prepared for or capable of this magnitude of energy. Instead, you are given bits and pieces. Each person is given that which he is capable of absorbing.

True, some are born with a consciousness that allows greater awareness. But, in the end, it really doesn't matter. What matters is that you live the life you were given in the best way possible.

SELF-AWARENESS

Some people believe that some animals are not self-aware, while humans are. Scientists love to test this in various species with mirrors and other gadgets. You, of course, test as more aware than many others. I would like to have your perspective on this.

First, there is no "right" or "wrong" here; not one definitive answer. If you begin to think you know something others do not and that you are right, you will shut yourself off to the opinions and perceptions of others. This is the death of curiosity, openness, and acceptance of those who are different from you. Of course, you know this, but still you tend to believe that what you receive from us is "ultimate truth." It cannot be. All is filtered through your own thoughts and perceptions, as well as your current level of consciousness and awareness. Therefore, everything you—or anyone else—receives is limited and not "ultimate truth."

Now, about self-awareness and what it means to us. We could feel your resistance to the idea that humans are self- aware while animals are not. This is because you *know* in your heart of hearts that we are no different from you at the level of the soul.

Yes, I know it is true. And so when anyone else implies otherwise, I am disturbed.

We are beings of God, just as you are. We too were created by the Master Creator, or Divine Consciousness. We are part of that energy, as are you and everything else in the universe. We are aware of who we are at a soul level, as you are.

Dearest one, people have discussed and debated this huge topic of self-awareness for a long time. Our way is not to confirm or dispel one idea or another.

As we've said, there is no ultimate truth.

But here is how we see it: like you, we live on Earth in physical bodies. Our bodies are not as refined as human bodies in many ways. Our brains are different. We were designed for different purposes.

Part of your function, as human beings, is to think, reflect, analyze, assess, and create. And because of this, your entire constitution is designed in a certain way.

Our function is different, as we have already described; our physical bodies, including our brains, are not attuned to the kind of awareness and thought processes to which humans are privy.

We know who and what we are, as elephants. But we do not reflect upon it, question it, judge it, assess it, or analyze it. This is the difference.

Could you reframe this, keeping it simple and straightforward?

At a soul level, all of us are made of the same substance—pure consciousness. There is no form and therefore no differentiation between us. We are all part of one great energy.

An energetic map or blueprint delineates the characteristics each form will have, as it comes into physical existence on Earth. For our purposes right now, let us call these forms "species." All right?

Yes.

So each species has an individual identity on Earth, but at the same time, is made of the same consciousness as all other species.

Got it.

Now, let us say that each different species has a different role to play on this planet. It is nourished by the same energy, or consciousness, and yet because the form is different, that energy is manifested differently. Still okay?

Yes.

Now let's say that Humanity's role here is to oversee the welfare of the planet, while, at the same time, learning lessons about love and peace. And let's say that because of this role, humans have certain challenges to face on the path of their own growth, as individuals and as a species.

Okay.

This is, perhaps, where the idea of dominion came from: that Humanity is responsible for the well-being and welfare of the planet. Like a CEO (chief executive officer) in a corporation who takes on a leadership role. So humanity is the CEO of this planet.

All right. This makes sense.

Because of this role, as CEOs of the Earth, people have certain abilities and functions. One is the potential awareness of what they are doing at all times, as well as awareness of what everyone and everything else is doing.

And from this awareness, they are able to incorporate the energy of every other being into their consciousness, if they are at a high enough level to do so.

It is much like the eagle who sees all, from a higher perspective. Humans have this ability in their highest state of awareness; to see all, and to know how to act on this awareness in order to bring peace and cooperation to all beings.

And how does this differ from your function here?

Humans, as we said, have responsibility for this planet and all beings who live here. We are more responsible for the Earth herself. We maintain and align the energy of the Earth in such a way that she is able to sustain all beings.

I am getting a sense that you work from the ground up, while Humanity works from above and downward. Is this accurate?

Partially. Let us explain further. Perhaps it is necessary to understand the function of Earth to understand what we and the Whales do.

This planet, Earth, has consciousness, which is different from that of other planets. One of her roles is to sustain life as you know it. And because of this, her consciousness is reflected in all beings who live here. In turn, the consciousness of all beings comes back to her. So it is a cycle of love, support, and awareness.

When harm is done to the Earth, it is felt throughout the consciousness of all beings inhabiting this planet. Conversely, when something of great benefit to the planet is accomplished, that too is sensed by all her inhabitants.

Humans have the capacity to create or destroy on a larger scale than any other beings. Because of this, they have greater responsibility to care for the Earth. This is their gift and their challenge.

Our responsibility is to care for the energetic integrity of the Earth. Through our focused intent to keep her in a state of love and harmony, we help the Earth retain this intention and it is reflected back to all beings.

When you speak of Humanity operating from above and us operating from below, it is a bit misleading and limiting; it all works together. However, it is true that we work from the Earth and out beyond, while you work from Spirit and down to all beings, which ultimately affects the welfare of the planet. But as there is no space and time in the spiritual realms, so there is no up and down. There is no hierarchy of anything. No better or worse, stronger or weaker. All simply is. All works together as one divine force of love.

Isn't there a hierarchy of Archangels and Ascended Masters? I have learned that these beings are of higher rank and oversee other angels and divine beings. They evidently are of a higher frequency or vibration than many others.

This is a subject we cannot get into. We do not operate at this level, and do not have awareness about how these realms operate.

It may be very true that there are hierarchies of divine beings. We do not want to address this because we don't know about it. But what we do know is that the souls of animals and humans are part of the same consciousness. No one is better or higher than another, just different. This is what we address here.

GUIDANCE

Can you please speak about divine guidance and prayer? Is this part of your reality?

Let's say there are two human friends walking in the woods. One has studied the Bible intensively and is aligned with its teachings. The other has studied Buddhism for many years, meditates regularly, and has had transcendent experiences.

Let's imagine they come to a stream to be crossed. The water is flowing rapidly and it is impossible to jump across; the stream is too wide. The person who has studied the Bible prays to Jesus and asks for help. The other one prays to Buddha and meditates in order to find a solution.

In the meantime, a stranger walks by and also wants to cross the stream. Rather than praying for help, he simply finds a big log, places it across the stream, and casually walks over it to the other side.

The two friends watch, puzzled. How could this happen? This man who has no obvious connection with higher guidance is able to cross the stream so easily while they are still asking for help.

Does this mean that Jesus and Buddha are not watching over them? Does it mean that they are not deep enough into their meditation and prayer to receive wise guidance? Certainly not.

Eventually they cross the stream, using the other man's log, and they continue to discuss the ramifications of this scenario. They come to see, because they are wise men, that the other man was no less spiritual, no less in touch with Spirit than they. While they sat waiting for clear guidance, he simply acted upon his own internal guidance, which manifested as a very simple act.

Sometimes divine guidance comes as a thought or insight, as a vision, as a dream. Sometimes it is just a way of interacting with the world from moment to moment, living one's life to its fullest. We are like that stranger, and humans have the potential to be the two friends. Had these friends waited a little longer, perhaps the thought of using a log to cross the stream would have come to one or both of them. Or perhaps there would have been another solution. There is that potential.

But the other man, the stranger, lived in harmony with his world. He simply knew what to do. Perhaps he was guided. Perhaps he had experience in these matters. Perhaps he had common sense and was a problem solver. It doesn't really matter.

We, as earth-bound, physical beings, have vast experience and knowledge available to us. We receive clear guidance constantly and consistently, and we are open to hearing it and acting upon it. However, we do not consciously pray for guidance. We simply live it.

You, as human beings, are able to ask for help, to pray, to meditate. You are capable of full awareness of your God-state. You can commune with the Divine, consciously. You have the intelligence, awareness, imagination, and the physical capacity to do things we cannot do.

This does not make you better or worse in our eyes. It does, however, confer upon you certain responsibilities. Consciously consider the consequences of your actions. Earth, as we know her, is in your hands.

CHAPTER 19

LIKE DUMBO

My friends, you have told me that you want to give me some new information and I am excited about that.

Yes. Our journey on Earth started a very long time ago. We came in different forms, some of which you are familiar with, such as mastodons and mammoths. There were others as well. We have an extensive history on this planet.

You may ask where we came from. We were not simply hatched! Our consciousness, of course, preceded us, before we took form.

What we want to share with you now is what that consciousness is about. As you know, we carry the intention to spread peace and harmony. We are a kind of glue that binds the Earth together via our footfalls and soundings that work with the grid lines of the Earth. We, along with the great Whales, have this mission.

However, there is more. We are interplanetary beings. A part of our conscious awareness is on Earth, but other aspects mingle with energies in far distant planes and realities. We want to share some of this with you so you might grasp a larger picture and perspective of who we are as souls.

Our star system is not a solid physical foundation like Earth; it is comprised of energy. Light and sound are energy, as you know. Our home is made of this kind of vibration.

How then do you embody on Earth if you are not in physical form originally?

Ah, a good question. And one that extends to you, as human. If you do not come from a place that is physical, how do you take form? And why?

Each form has certain characteristics and functions. All work together as part of a greater whole. It is like a giant jigsaw puzzle, where all the parts fit together and create a beautiful design. If one part is missing, the entire puzzle doesn't work as well. And if a number of pieces are missing, the whole thing may collapse.

So it is on planet Earth. As more and more species die out, the puzzle, that is the Earth plane, can malfunction and eventually collapse. It is critically important now to let people know the dangers of ignoring or decimating parts of this planet. This includes animal and plant species, as well as aspects of the Earth herself: the waters and the land.

We carry within us, within our soul aspect, a certain energetic imprint. A certain vibration. Ours is a deep, expansive one. We carry a quality of wisdom and knowledge that extends beyond most humans' capacity to comprehend. That is why this is hard for you to translate.

Please simplify this or give me a metaphor or story for better understanding. Not specific details, but maybe a bigger picture of who you are as souls and what you carry?

Do you remember the story of Dumbo, the flying elephant? This adorable little elephant is able to fly because he is light of heart, like a little angel. He is a large, heavy being able to soar like a bird and bring joy to many.

Yes, it is a wonderful children's story. What does that have to do with you?

This story is fantasy with a relic of truth. As weighty embodied elephants, of course, we cannot fly. However, our consciousness, our soul essence, can be anywhere anytime. We can move from place to place, reality to reality, dimension to dimension, in the flash of a thought. So, in a sense, we can fly!

Because of our depth of intelligence and heartfulness, we love to explore different realities and see what works, what doesn't, what is possible, what has been, and what can be created. We have a wealth of knowledge about how beings live and operate in other systems.

Our life on Earth is not easy, nor is it easy for most beings on this planet. That is for good reason. We are here to learn and grow; without challenges, we can't evolve. We become complacent.

Other dimensions and realities have challenges, but not the same ones and, often, not as difficult. So there is growth of a different sort. We are fascinated by this and we explore what works and what doesn't.

LIGHT BEINGS

Your vision of Elephants of Light in the sky was an accurate and powerful one. This is who we are. We are light beings, as you are. Our earthly bodies are temporary aspects of a divine essence of light, love, and peace.

You may wonder why we choose these massive bodies with strange protrusions, like trunks and tails. What is the purpose? Why have we chosen to incarnate in such a manner?

Our trunk is our antenna. It is our means of relating to the world. It is a sensory organ, a communication instrument, and a sensitive part of our body. It is a useful tool, and it serves us well.

Our tail is small and seemingly insignificant, and yet it protects our rear from harmful things that might invade our bodies.

Our massive size has massive impact. Our consciousness is large and expansive and requires a large body to project our energy outward.

What is this energy that you carry and need to project?

We have shared with you our intention and purpose on Earth. But where does that energy come from originally? That is what we address now: the source.

When we were born out of stardust and divine consciousness, we were given certain characteristics that we hold dear. Great minds. Deep hearts and compassion. A large capacity to hold, maintain, and disperse energy. This has evolved over time as we have inhabited these great bodies in various forms and in different dimensions.

Earth is one of our favorites. Certainly it is more challenging than many others. But it is fascinating and we learn a great deal as we live this existence. Human beings are perhaps our greatest challenge but also our great teachers. Even in your blunders—and there are many— we learn from you. What to do, how to be, and how not to be, what not to do.

In other realities, the teachings are not always as clear. So we are grateful to Humanity for the teachings you offer. Not always easy, but always instructive.

CHAPTER 20

GUIDANCE FOR BUSINESS OWNERS

I was invited to ask the Elephants to speak to a conference of professional business people. Here is what they said:

We are honored to speak with you. We want to work with you to create a much healthier planet. We can't do the physical labor but we can certainly add our energy and support to what you do. Call on us for that.

Can you please give some practical advice?

First, do no harm. This has been a tenet of medical practice for a long time and it applies here as well. If you consider that what you do could have harmful effects on the environment or beings who live there, please reconsider. This is important.

Second, consider who you might help with your actions. It is not enough to do good things for a few human beings, although that is commendable. Consider reaching beyond your current limitations and do what might benefit others—humans, animals, plant life, and the Earth herself.

It is time for humans to reach beyond their own self-concerns and take into account the lives of other beings, including other humans that may not be directly affected by your product or service.

For instance, you might think about using some of the funds you receive to support others, through charitable endeavors. Or you might produce a by-product that could serve other uses than that for which it was originally intended.

You could think about how you treat your employees. You might create a cooperative environment for them. They then may feel honored and privileged to volunteer their efforts as a community, to support others locally or globally. This could create a mutually beneficial environment for the people who work together as a team, and also for those they serve.

Consider, please, restoring habitat. So much is being lost and we, as animals, suffer greatly from this. Our lands are being taken. Our air is polluted, as are the great waters. Our beautiful trees are cut down so we have no place to go, no way to sustain ourselves. We need people to stop the slaughter of animals and habitat. Through your ethical business practices, you can help in this way. You have power to do this that we do not have. Please help us in this way and we will be eternally grateful.

CHAPTER 21

CLIMATE CHANGE

Please tell me about Climate Change and Global Warming. People haven't taken it seriously enough for many years and now the earth changes are happening. Fires, floods, hurricanes, tsunamis. Serious droughts. Habitats are changing which directly affect animals and plants. It seems to be caused by humans but is not affecting only humans. The entire world is at risk, and our leaders are not doing enough to stop it. It certainly impacts you as well, with not enough food to eat in places, lack of water, and other problems. How do you see this issue? Do you have any advice for humans?

Thank you for asking. It is an important topic. We cannot, of course, influence human activity that is creating much of this problem in the first place. It is not possible and we wouldn't choose to do it anyway. This issue is part of human evolution. But we can speak about our view of this situation.

What we see is that human beings have become more and more disconnected from the Earth and the natural world. Not only that, but disconnected from themselves and their higher nature, that divine spark that knows exactly how to protect Earth and all beings. Without that love affair with the natural world, humans have greedily sought to meet their own needs with complete disregard for the world around them. And so now our seas and skies are polluted, many beings are being eliminated, and our world has changed dramatically—and continues to do so.

This is not news, of course. We only tell you what we see and sense. But you know all of this.

For us, climate change is part of a much larger problem. It is one element in a deteriorating planet, mostly human caused. And because humans have created this, they are the ones who can change that trajectory. But only if they choose to do so.

We are not as concerned about this as many of you seem to be. We know that we are here as part of a divine plan and what befalls the planet befalls us. If we die, we move on into other realms of existence. We are not worried or dismayed about that. But what we do feel and know is that as our blessed Earth is destroyed and species leave, the precious gift we have been given will no longer exist and that makes us extremely sad.

We too suffer the consequences of these dramatic shifts in our climate and the changes that come about as a result. Life becomes even harder for many of us. So we do not take this lightly.

But if we speak as Souls, not physical elephants, we have a different perspective. You, as a species, have such tremendous potential and you are blowing it. As many of you, and many of your leaders, succumb to greed, arrogance, and self-centered desires, you set a course bound for destruction.

The climate is only one aspect of many that need to be addressed, and soon. We try our best to bring peace and tranquility to Earth, but we can only do so much. It is up to you.

This sounds a lot like doomsday talk. I need something positive and hopeful from you. And some practical advice. None of us have the capacity to change all of humankind. But what actions can we take, as individual humans who care, to help reverse the course we are on?

First, dear one, we did not intend to give such a negative picture. But these are scary times and we feel it too. So let's change direction now and focus on what's good and right, and how we can change this.

We remind you now of your vision of Elephants in the sky, and the positive, loving light that we shed upon the Earth. This vision is real. As real as what you see before your eyes as a person living on our lovely planet. The "unseen" world is as valid as the one you see with your two eyes.

You can't imagine how many beings are working on your behalf. Not only earthly beings, which includes animals and plants, especially the great Trees. But also numerous other beings that live in the Spirit world. Some of these are earth-based elementals and nature spirits. Others are high spirit-based beings, some from other realms or other worlds. All here to help Humanity and Earth evolve in consciousness. You are truly not alone.

What you see in your media is a dark picture based in fear. But so much more is happening that is not emphasized in the media. Large and small acts of kindness. People taking action in so many ways to further equality and justice on all levels. Others acting on behalf of animals, nature, and the Earth herself to repair what has been damaged. This movement, dearest sister, is as great as that which is projected through your television and computer screens. Simply unreported. And it is growing. Every day, new people join in.

This is wonderful, but still, many leaders, as well as great numbers of their followers, are doing terrible things. What can I do, as one person in a population of 8 billion?

You do what you are doing, what you are guided to do. How do you know what that is? You simply pay attention to what feels good and right in your heart, your mind, and your body. These callings from our inner core, our divine nature, are getting stronger now.

What might have seemed hidden before is right in front of you. Every individual has a different task. You can pretend you don't know what that is, but in the end, the call will be so strong, you can no longer deny it.

You don't have to change the world. In fact, you can't. Not alone. But your efforts combined with the work of many others can truly make a great difference. Your part may seem small and insignificant, but it is not. Each piece of the puzzle counts.

Is there anything more you want to say about climate change?

Our Earth wants to work WITH you, not against you. Whatever you do to the Earth, you do to yourselves. If your energy is dense and negative, that will be projected back to you. This holds true for the collective as well as the individual. So do your best to project positive, loving energy. As you do this, so will others. And you create an entire movement that can't help but impact the Earth and all her life forms. We truly are all in this together, so let's work together for a better world.

Thank you, beloved friends. May it be so.

We sense that now humanity is at a turning point. You can choose to live or die. To live, you must change old patterns and beliefs that have created a multitude of systems that simply don't work.

Change requires energy, dedication, effort, and a shift in consciousness. There is a period when the old clearly does not work any longer, but the new has not yet settled in. That is where you are now.

There are many people fighting for change, waking up, having the courage to say, "NO MORE" to the old order. But these outmoded ways of being are deeply entrenched in human consciousness, and some people are holding tightly to them. Fighting for their lives, actually. So they are fierce and determined, and will do their best to stop anyone and anything that stands in their way.

As people wake up to the truth of what has been happening on this planet, and they then stand up and speak out, more and more love, peace, and joy will sweep through the Earth. But how many people will actually stand up?

By standing up we do not mean that people need to protest or fight. We mean stand up to their own inner conscience and values. Honor the truth of what they know in their deepest being. Spread love rather than hatred, peace rather than chaos, compassion rather than judgment.

It is happening. We see it, feel it, and know it. There is hope for this world, and right now is the time for change, for transformation. Spread light, love, compassion, peace, joy, and hope to all you see every day. This will change everything.

CHAPTER 22

HEALING THE EARTH

I have researched and thought about your infrasounds and how you detect them. You told me you can sense other elephants this way, and send them signals when they are far away. Your rumbling and footsteps create these sounds.

This raises a question. You have told me often that you work with the grid lines of the Earth; you stabilize and harmonize the energy of the Earth this way. Are these infrasonic sounds what impact the Earth in this manner?

The Earth is made of energy, as is everything. You have discovered that the vibrations we produce can be contained within certain parameters that have various names in human language: infrasounds, Rayleigh waves, etc. We don't know names but we can sense what is happening. This is what we will describe to you.

When we move on the Earth, there is an impact. The immediate impact most easily detectable by human instruments is on the surface of the Earth. But the actions we take have far reaching consequences that go beyond the surface, deep into the Earth herself. We have a strong alliance with the Earth and she is sensitive to our vibrations, our energy. She responds to us, as we respond to her messages as well. It is a two way street, so to speak.

Because our intention is for healing and stabilization, she receives this and turns it into her own supportive energy. When we vocalize or send vibrations through our feet, the Earth receives them.

What does this do for the Earth? How is she impacted and how does she respond?

Here's an analogy. Say, you have a ball. The size of a basketball. You hold it in your hands, you bounce it, you throw it, you catch it. This is how you manipulate the ball. The ball responds to your touch as well as your intention. If your intention is to throw the ball, your arms respond and the ball follows. There is no thought process in the ball. It simply responds to the action you take.

It is much the same with the way we interact with the Earth. She too is a ball, a very large one. Although she is conscious, there are physical processes that occur that she has no direct influence or control over. She simply responds.

We send energy to the Earth to balance and attune her to all the energies that surround her. It is our way of protecting The Mother, our home planet. We have come here for this purpose: to stabilize not only the physical Earth, but all the beings who live within and on the surface.

Because we are large creatures and have the capacity to create powerful sound waves, or waves of energy, we are able to transmit these vibrations into the Earth along with our intent for healing, integration, synchronization, and alignment. And she receives that energy and takes it in.

What does this have to do with the grid lines? And what do you mean specifically by grid lines? It seems they are different from ley lines, that have been described as connecting sacred sites. Is this so?

Yes, these energy lines, or grids, encircle the Earth. They are part of the composition of the Earth's energy blueprint. They are like the batting in a quilt, forming stable barriers that contain energy and keep it from drifting or flowing. Thus, these grids create more strength and stability. So when we say that we work with the grid lines, it means that we are helping to hold the energy in place and therefore stabilize, support, and balance the planet.

Our work is now more important than ever. The Earth and all life here is in danger. People need to know this information.

Why?

Because, dearest one, we work with humans to restore the Earth to a sustainable level. She is suffering and all her creatures are suffering. This must end if life is to continue as we know it. The animals are a piece of this great puzzle and people must acknowledge that. We have systems and mechanisms to help humanity heal this planet. The rampant, unconscious killing must end. Not only of animals, but people as well. Violence has become a way of life for many humans and this cannot continue. Greed, ignorance, and violence must end. By connecting with us and other forces of nature, people can heal and go on to live more productive, conscious, loving lives. It is no longer a luxury. It is a necessity.

CHAPTER 23

EARTH'S ASCENSION

What can you tell me about Earth's ascension to a higher vibration, or higher state of consciousness?

From our perspective, the Earth will ascend as Humanity ascends. The two are intertwined.

What does this mean?

As our Mother Earth evolves, so do human beings and all living creatures that inhabit her. We are all related, all connected. Part of the great experiment here is the evolution of Humanity. Humans are fairly primitive beings. We are here to help you evolve in consciousness. If humans cannot transcend the greed, manipulation, and self-centered way of being, they will destroy themselves and probably take most life on Earth with them. If, however, they can change their way of life, and change it enough to prevent catastrophe, all will change and move into a higher vibration, a higher consciousness.

My understanding is that Earth is evolving into a higher or more refined vibration regardless of what we, as humans, do. It is our choice to evolve with her or not. Some say that Earth is moving into the 5th dimension from the 3rd, and there is energy and support from higher beings to help us in this process. Still, many people adhere strongly to the old ways and refuse to change. So it is unclear what will happen to Humanity over time. Can you speak about this? What do you see?

We have seen civilizations thrive and others die out, not only on Earth, but on many other planets, star systems, and dimensions. It is, in part, why we are here: to help Humanity. But ultimately, the choice is yours.

In one way, you are correct in saying that the Earth will evolve, regardless of what human beings do. You can evolve with her or perish. But from our perspective, this is not totally accurate. Let us explain.

This planet, our beautiful Mother Earth, came into existence in order to nurture and sustain all living beings that choose to inhabit her. Sometimes those beings will cease to exist. They no longer fit into the evolutionary wave taking place. New beings may replace them, ones that can survive in a new environment, or new energy—however you want to see it.

Civilizations come and go. Species come and go. Life forms come and go. This is simply how it works.

You, meaning humans currently embodied, often see yourselves as the top of the line, the most superior creatures. For this reason, you often feel immune to the forces of nature that may challenge your very existence. It is this arrogance, this sense of entitlement, that may be the source of your destruction. When you refuse to acknowledge that you are not the highest possible beings that have been created, and you disregard the tremendous gifts and blessings you have been given, you deny your own potential for evolving into an entirely new kind of person. One who shares the Earth with all life in a grateful, respectful, loving way.

By this we do not mean to imply that Earth is evolving and humans are simply reflections of that process. No. Humans are part of it. The forces that support Earth's evolution support Human evolution as well. Not separate and not either/or. And, beloved Human Beings, always the choice is yours. To go with the flow or resist and get stuck in the mud.

Thank you. This makes sense to me. And how do you fit in with this?

Yes, yes, yes! Thank you for asking. We too are evolving, as is every living being. But we do not resist as many humans do. We simply accept what is.

So what does this mean? What if Humanity destroys itself and we take you along with us? Or what if we die and you live on?

You humans so love to project into the future, and you want to know everything. It makes life hard sometimes, does it not? We live in the present and do our best to accept each step as it comes. We know, ultimately, that the Universe, or the Divine, is benevolent. We know that we go on even after these fragile bodies die. So what happens next here is not our concern. There is not much we can do about it anyway. We simply surrender to what is and live each moment, just as it comes.

Thank you so much. I wish I could be more like you and stop the worrying and constant analyzing and trying to understand. It is draining.

It is part of what makes you human. The other side of worry, the positive aspect, is caring about what happens and potentially taking action to create a better future. Please don't berate yourself for being exactly who and what you are. Use that concern to promote change.

HOME

Can you tell me more about where you come from, your home base?

Yes, we come from a world without conflict, where there are no physical bodies, only energetic forms. Like the Elephants you saw in the sky, we live in those light bodies, not limited to any one time or place. We live in the Spirit realms where time and space don't exist in the way they do on Earth. We don't inhabit one planet or place, as you know it. We congregate in a particular dimension. We were born in this place that is not a place. It is an energy, an environment that suits our needs.

What does that mean? Are there other beings with you? Do other animals live in the same way and then come to Earth? Don't you have a particular home base?

Yes, but not a "place" as you know places. It is more nebulous than a particular area. We can move from place to place easily. We are not locked in to any one region or planet or star. Yet we congregate together. Other beings, some of which become animals on Earth, associate with us. We are deeply familiar with many of the animals we live with on Earth.

We also know humans, but from afar. We have studied and watched you from a distance and we know who you are. We consciously chose to inhabit this planet, specifically to help you and all beings evolve in consciousness. As we all evolve together, the consciousness of Earth, our home, evolves as well. She consciously invited humans to live on her so we all might grow together. She is generous that way.

She knew, as did we, that this would not be an easy journey. But it is a delight to watch humans evolve and we wanted that for this great planet. All creatures joined in, some more conscious than others about the task at hand, but all highly committed to their own and the Earth's evolution.

It seems I have known you in other dimensions. Is this true? Did I come from the same place, or situation, as you did?

Of course, that's our deep, strong connection. In your language, we are soul mates. We cross dimensions of reality easily. We, and you, are energetic beings at our core. This is why you have struggled to determine where you come from. It is not a place. It is a state of being. And so, yes, we know one another well.

OUR EVOLUTION

I would like to go back to the initial question about Earth's ascension and humanity's evolution. Some say that as we awaken to higher spiritual dimensions, our DNA is changing and we will become a different species altogether. One that is of a higher, less dense frequency. Some speak of us having a crystalline matrix. Can you speak about this?

As we see it, we evolve together and, as we do, of course our bodies change; not in shape or even much that is seen outwardly. What it means is that our internal framework becomes more refined. We speak about light, and our light bodies; that which we ultimately become as we leave this plane of existence. But, even on Earth, our bodies can become more light-filled. As density diminishes, light enters.

So what is light really? What do you mean by this? I just looked it up online and found this from Johns Hopkins University:

"Simply stated, light is nature's way of transferring energy through space. We can complicate it by talking about interacting electric and magnetic fields, quantum mechanics, and all of that, but just remember—light is energy."

So, light is energy. Everything is energy. But when you speak about "becoming light" and losing the physical body, what does that mean? I don't need to know in terms of physics. I simply want to know what it means to lose density, become light, and embody a higher consciousness.

Okay. Let's go.

Our origin is pure energy. Light is pure energy. Sound is pure energy. When we embody on Earth, we take on the density, the weight, the structure, of physical form. In simple terms, when we lose some of that density, the light returns to fill the "empty" space. Actually, it doesn't enter. It already exists. It is just covered over by something more visible to the embodied senses. Light is always there.

Light is often equated with love. What does that mean? How does it work?

Love is the primary force in the universe. It is what causes life to flourish. It is the glue that holds everything together. This force that many call God, Creator, Source, All That Is, is the essence of love. Love is what creates and it also destroys something that no longer serves its Divine purpose. So love is the foundation of the cosmos.

Then why is light associated with love?

When we say "light" we mean the energy that is always present. And that energy's essence is love.

When we speak about elevating consciousness, or raising vibration, we speak of releasing some of the heaviness, or density, of physical structure so that light, or love, prevails. Does this make sense now?

Yes, thank you. I know I have asked some difficult questions but I want to understand. I know that, at the soul level, you are truly my teachers. It is simply unfathomable to me that people don't "get" who you are. Some even see you as "dumb animals." What a great loss for them!

We want to explain something to you, dear Barbara.

When we first came into being on this planet, we took on bodies that were new to us. It was part of the contract we made with that magnanimous being called Earth. These forms allowed us to walk on her body and be fully present to the gifts she had to share: her resources, her energies, her empowerment. In turn, our promise was to love and care for her in the best way we could.

Humans have disrupted that contract. I feel so sad about that, and guilty for being human.

There is no need to feel guilty, dearest one. Do not take on the entire responsibility of humanity. You are one person and your heart is open. Your intention is strong to heal what has been broken. So please don't take this on.

It is true that we also feel sad about what is happening. But we know there is still hope for humanity and all life here. It requires a shift in attitude. From our perspective, that is already happening. Many people are waking up to current reality.

Now, back to the original contract. As we have said, many beings have come and gone from our precious Mother Earth. There will continue to be a "changing of the guard" and shifting consciousness as long as there is life on Earth. Some will adapt and others will not. And that is really, truly okay.

Time has accelerated. We all feel it. The shift in consciousness is speeding up because our Mother, the Earth, needs us now. All of the universe is conspiring to aid in this great shift: calling in light, calling in love, calling in higher awareness.

It is not an easy transition. So much has already been set in place that it is hard to remove and replace these energies. But it is surely possible, and is necessary if we are all to survive. And we will. In the end, we will all know who and what we are at the deepest level. We will honor Earth again. We will honor one another. We will know ourselves as Souls, even within these finite bodies.

You have told me that you don't think about past or future, that you live in the present. But this seems to be a strong future vision. How do you explain that?

We do not think about the future as we live in these physical bodies. We live day by day. However, at the soul level—which is where we speak from now—we hold a strong vision and intent for a much brighter future on Earth. We see it and know it. And we ask you to do the same, for the benefit of all life on Earth.

Thank you my great beloved teachers, sages, and friends. Thank you.

CHAPTER 24

FUTURE VISION

There was a time in history when humans and non-human animals shared one consciousness. In that time, our language was subtle and nonverbal. It was all that was needed. As time went on, our language remained the same, but yours changed. And as your language became more complicated, so did your lifestyle.

Yes, our lifestyle has become so complex and convoluted that many are unhappy, our world is disappearing as we have known it, and there is great turmoil and unrest. Violence reigns in many areas. People are starving, while others exploit them even more. There is hunger, disease, and depression in our human world. And now the climate is changing as a result of human interference.

As a result of your human attitude and actions, our Elephant world is changing as well. We no longer have enough supportive habitat.

Many of us are held captive in your zoos and parks, or as "beasts of burden." Others are dying from unconscious human behavior. It is not a happy situation.

What to do? We can complain and get angry, as many of us do. The outrage is enormous. This pent-up anger can be very destructive.

But there is another way; through peace and understanding. In your world many teach and promote peace, freedom, love, and all kinds of beautiful things. Many follow these teachings. As the numbers increase, which is happening daily, peace will reign. It is hard to imagine this because of all the war and violence in your world, but we see it as true. We know it.

My vision is to have a world where all beings live together in peace and harmony. Is this even possible?

Ahhhh, peace.

Peace is what we all strive for. We, as Earth inhabitants, have a dual nature within us. We cannot live as only spiritual beings, or we wouldn't be here in bodies. And because of this duality, we are forced, in a sense, to express all of our emotions and all of who we are. Otherwise, there is tension, disharmony, and frustration.

It is certainly possible to have a planet of peace and harmony, where love is the predominant force. However, in order to attain this, there is a need to express all of who we are: the dark as well as the light. There needs to be an acceptance of this and an honoring of it, such that space is provided—physical space, emotional space, mental space, and spiritual space—allowing each individual to experience and express the full range of emotion, creativity, and then to live life as it is.

An ideal world, where all live in peace, yes. A world of complacency, without fire and passion, no. There needs to be a balance of all elements, all personalities, all species, all that is. No longer can any aspect of anyone or anything be denied or ignored. All must be accepted, honored, and nurtured with love. Only then can we all live in peace.

Stop thinking about how terrible war is and feeling angry at those you perceive as creating it; focus instead on what this world *could* be.

Based on memory and clear vision, we foresee a world where all beings, including humans, live in harmony. There is no separation or judgment. Only love and peace prevail. In this world, we all speak the same language, a language of the heart and soul. There is understanding and communication at all levels at all times. There is no hierarchy. All beings are seen as and treated as equal. We each have our own contribution, and every gift is well honored and respected.

We dance the dance of life as one happy family. No one goes hungry. No one envies another or fights for possession of anything or anyone. The unseen world is perceived as real and tangible, just as much as the physical world you now recognize. Angels, fairies, and nature spirits are accessible and honored. No one questions the reality of anything or anyone else. Love, peace, harmony, and joy infuse our world. This day will come, as long as we all create it together.

Thank you, great ones. I surely hope so.

Hoping doesn't work, not alone. Action—meaning spiritual action—does work. It is about visualizing and *feeling* peace every day. By living in peace, others receive this as well and go on to spread it to others. This is the way of creation. This is the blessing of creation. You humans are not alone in your ability to create. We all have that power. And if we can do this as a united force, this world will be changed forever.

Epilogue

In July 2022, I did something I had dreamed of for many years: I went to Botswana. For me, it is the epicenter of African wilderness, with fewer people and lots of animals. A true experience of the bush. I had been to East and South Africa before. In fact, I had lived in Kenya for a year. But Botswana always called.

So, I organized a safari in 2019, all set to go in 2020. Then the pandemic hit, and I had to postpone my trip for two years. Finally, in 2022, I got to go. HOORAY! Hallelujah!

Not only did I go to Botswana, I went on a mobile tented safari. This means I lived in a tent for two weeks, rather than staying in lodges as many people do. Now, that's probably not a big deal, but I hadn't been camping for several years. I've gotten older in these last few years since I set up this trip, and I really was a little concerned. However, it was one of the best experiences of my life. I loved every moment of it, even the challenges. Actually, the challenges often became gifts.

No electricity, no cell phones, no computers, no news, no running water or indoor toilets. The gift? Pure air, absolute peace, and quiet time to reflect and enjoy amazing people and magnificent animals. We saw an enormous variety of animal species, and to my great delight, lots of babies—lions, wild dogs, zebras, giraffes, impala and other kinds of antelopes, baboons, and, of course, elephants.

And it was cold! One would think that Africa is hot, but this was July, the middle of winter below the equator, and it was certainly cold at night and in the mornings. Getting out of my warm, comfy bed, I would brace myself for the cold, donning five layers of clothing to start the day. And often a large poncho to top it off, for the breezy, early morning game drives. But by noon, it all came off except the bottom layers because it was quite warm in the African sun. But then, when the sun set and the brilliantly colored sky covered the landscape, I had to put all those layers back on. The gift? Sitting by a warm fire at night and eating delicious food prepared by our wonderful staff over an open fire. They even made fresh bread and cakes each day. I can't imagine how they did it.

This was the first time I got to meet Avantika, my podcast cohost, in person! We had been doing zoom calls for a couple years, initially with long conversations and later to create our marvelous podcast, *Animals and Us: Voices of a New Paradigm.* In Africa we finally met, face to face. So that too was a great blessing of this journey.

Botswana is such a special place, where elephants roam free in large numbers. The peacefulness and contentment I felt in their presence was something I will always carry with me. This is life as it should be, for all elephants everywhere. Not in cages. Not confined. Not performing. Not restricted or controlled in any way, but wild and free.

I was surprised by how many bulls there were. They were scattered throughout the country, as I saw later from a small plane. A bull here, a bull there, hanging out, eating grass, solitary for the most part. I did see some cows and babies, and that was fabulous, but primarily it was the bulls. And they were especially prevalent, it seems, in the Delta.

Okavango Delta is a huge expanse of waterways, created by water that flows in each year from the Angolan highlands. It floods the northern part of Botswana and creates streams and rivulets that meander extensively. The Okavango Delta is 6,000 square kilometers (2,316 square miles). However, when the floodwaters arrive in the winter months from March to September, the Delta triples in size, to about 15,000 square kilometers (5,791 square miles). It is enormous.

I loved gliding through the water in a mokoro, which is like a flat canoe. Originally, they were made of wood, but now most are metal. They are propelled through the shallow waters of the delta by a person standing in the back of the boat and pushing with a long pole. Sometimes we got stuck and the driver had to get out and pull or push the mokoro or take turns doing both. But it was always a serene, sweet experience that allowed us to get very close to the elephants, as well as other wildlife. There were birds galore. Often racing through the water were herds of lechwe, an antelope species that lives in shallow waterways.

What was simply fascinating to me was the way the elephants living in the Delta would stand in the water, pluck out tall grasses with their trunks, swirl them around in big circles, water flying everywhere, and then eat the cleansed vegetation. Over and over and over again, for hours.

Being in the Delta, looking at a vast expanse of greenery and water, with very few people around, was probably the most peaceful scene I have ever seen in my life.

Seeing so many elephants in their natural habitat was, for me, a grand finale for this book. I was able to see them in action, and to learn more about who they are as physical beings. I could appreciate their tremendous contribution to their environment.

It's true that elephants can be extremely destructive. I saw many examples of trees that had been torn down or damaged. But, on the other hand, I witnessed the service this provides for other animals and plants. I saw seedlings blooming and growing after elephants had defecated in an area, so new life was sprouting from their waste. I saw baboons sitting together, plowing through elephant poop, picking out fruit and seeds that they gobbled down. I saw how many animals prospered from downed trees and open spaces. Bees, other insects, and birds inhabited those dead trees. I learned that elephants, as a keystone species, are truly remarkable environmental engineers, making way for myriad animals and plants to benefit from their activities.

One of the greatest gifts I received from being with elephants in Botswana was a completely different personal perspective about elephants on the ground. From my home in the US, I am bombarded with news about how elephants are being poached, how their population is declining, and how dreadful the current situation and the prospects for the future are for elephants.

I recently read that, according to the 2021 report by the International Union for Conservation of Nature, Africa's savanna elephant population declined by at least 60 percent over the last 50 years, while forest elephants declined by more than 86 percent over the past 31 years. Currently savanna elephants are listed as "endangered", while forest elephants are "critically endangered." Previously, both subspecies were listed as "vulnerable." Poaching and habitat loss are two of the leading contributors to this decline.

I find this abominable. Even in Botswana, hunting has been allowed. It can be overwhelmingly depressing. But that is not the whole story. I witnessed many lovely, seemingly contented elephants. Bull elephants were everywhere, solitary males munching on grasses for hour after hour. Cows and their little babies traveled together in small herds. To see these elegant animals, so at ease, calmed my own heart. It is still possible, still happening.

This is not to say that elephants are not in danger in many places, and not to discount in any way the vast numbers that have been killed for their tusks, captured for human entertainment, or displaced by human encroachment on their territories. But this experience gave me great hope that wild elephants can still live wild lives. Free and unencumbered.

As human beings, we have the capacity to facilitate this way of life, not only for elephants, but for all living creatures. We were given our miraculous brains, hearts, and hands for a reason. We can do this! But it takes dedication, commitment, and great compassion to make it happen. If it is possible for some, it is possible for all. These blessed beings that I encountered, living lives of joy and freedom, are precious examples of how life can be for all beings, including us. For me, this is true hope and inspiration for the future.

I came back changed from this trip, this great adventure. I knew something was happening to me when I was there, but I had no idea what that really meant until I got home and had some time to settle in, integrate my experiences, and do some contemplation and soul searching. What I now realize is that I am a different person. Several people I know have confirmed this, saying I look different now, more alive, and happier.

What does that really mean? For me, it means that I am more peaceful and self-assured. I took in the pure, vibrant energy of the place, of course, but in large part, this calm confidence, I believe, came from the elephants. These enormous animals can stand for hours and hours at a time, just munching on grass or slowly drinking water. And the peace they exude is contagious.

So, from being in their presence, I could feel the essence of who they are. While I was there, I did not communicate with them for the most part because I was so immersed in my own experience. But there was one time when I was in the vehicle, along with Avantika and seven others. We were very close to an elephant who was standing by a small pool of water, drinking at his leisure. At about the same moment, both Avantika and I received a very similar message directly from the elephant. He told us that we, as human beings, need to care for the earth.

What a profound message that was, and how true. And it reminded me of the deep interconnection we have with all life and with our great Mother Earth. And because we can, it is our responsibility to do all in our power to take care of our beloved home and all the beings who live within her realm.

I believe that part of the change in me is a deeper commitment to doing what I can to retain that peace inside of me, and to take on more responsibility to care for others and the Earth. I know I am not going to save anything or anyone by myself, but if I, and we, can work in conjunction with others of like-mind, like-spirit, and like-heart, I know we can make a huge difference on this great planet. And in doing so we will help not only ourselves as human beings, but all other creatures and lifeforms that inhabit this world.

If there is anything I would want from writing this book, it is that the deep, profound wisdom of these mighty, loving beings be projected out into the world for people to grasp, integrate, and then, perhaps, contribute in some way to the well-being of elephants and all life on Earth. A simple request, no? Let's make it so.

A FINAL MESSAGE FROM THE ELEPHANTS

Beloved Elephants,

I feel so blessed and privileged to have been with elephants in their own natural environment in Botswana, and to experience the calm demeanor that those elephants carry. But right now, the Earth is going through a lot of chaos and turbulence. Storms, fires, and floods worldwide. The climate is changing, in large part due to human influence. Many lives are being greatly disrupted and devastated. It all seems so tragic. I also know that the Earth is going through some big energy shifts that affect us all. Do you have any insight about this?

Yes, we do, in fact. Because we are so attuned to the Earth energies, we can speak to this question.

Our Mother Earth is indeed going through magnanimous changes. New energy is coming into our world that seems disruptive and chaotic, but that is because a great shift in universal consciousness is happening. A new consciousness is awakening and everyone in its path needs to surrender, and change, or possibly die.

It is a tremendous opportunity for new energy to supersede the old. For centuries, perhaps millennia, Earth has been subject to a strong energy of duality, which has often led to human conflict. An aura of competition and greed. Bigotry and violence. We, as animals, have often suffered the consequences of these actions and attitudes.

But now, our great Mother has said, "Enough!" It is time for a change. She can no longer tolerate the consequences of humankind's lack of care and responsibility. And so, Earth energy is shifting, often resulting in violent upheavals. This is what we are seeing worldwide.

As we said earlier, when referring to natural disasters, it is a matter of perception. Of course, if you are deeply affected by these Earth changes, you are not likely to see the blessing. You just want your life back. But there may be a bigger picture if you can see it that way.

If you consider that it is possible for the entire consciousness on Earth to transform into a way of being that no longer supports violence or hatred, you might then be able to tolerate the great revolution that is taking place. Even if there is death and destruction along the way.

So, dearest one, we cannot give you advice that will make this transition easier, unless you consider that knowing the larger picture can be a comfort when the situation feels unbearable. May this be a help for you and others.

Yes, thank you so much. I only hope that this chaos can end soon, and people will finally go along with the flow and stop resisting change so strongly. There are many now who hold fast to the old negative energies. That makes it very challenging. I wish I could say that I understand, and I have compassion for these people, but I get angry. It seems that in the human world now there is a very strong "us against them" mentality, and I must admit that I share some of this hostility toward people who are so filled with hatred, judgment, bigotry, and narrow-mindedness. I try to be less judgmental, but it is hard right now.

We understand. It is hard to be compassionate when you feel like you are being attacked or are watching others being abused or discriminated against. Yes, we understand this very well. But it all comes back to inner peace. Tend to your own wounds first. And recognize that those who hate others must hate themselves first. Otherwise, they would not carry such anger. Love yourself, live in a harmonious state, and continue to promote peace and understanding. Eventually, this becomes your reality, no matter what others do or say.

We want to remind you of something. You have it ALL inside. Love, hate, anger, peace, freedom, confinement, joy, despair. It is up to you what you do with these sentiments. Will you use them to destroy or to build? Will you use them for good or evil? Will you love yourself and enjoy your life, or will you choose to be angry and resentful? The choice is yours.

Enormous shifts are taking place on this planet, and it is not an easy process. However, if you can embody the good and help others with love and compassion, your life can be magnificent, no matter what is happening around you.

Of course, you grieve the losses. You must allow the more difficult emotions to move through you. But in the end, by living your own joyful, loving life, you influence others to do the same. Do not feel guilty about your own happiness. It truly is contagious.

We have been delighted to work on this book. It has been our pleasure. To have our voice heard is a true blessing, and to share that with others who might benefit increases the blessing multifold. So, thank you for joining us. May the loving conversations we have shared here serve as a model for you to do the same, but in your own way. It is these kinds of connections and communications that will make this world a much better, kinder, and more sustainable place in which to live.

About the Author

In 1992, Barbara Shor left veterinary practice and has been an animal communicator ever since. This book is an updated and expanded version of the elephant portion of her first book, *Soul of the Wild: Intimate Messages from the Hearts and Souls of Elephants and Whales,* incorporating inspiring new ideas and perspectives.

Barbara graduated from Colorado State University veterinary school in 1983. After working in private practice for a few years, she then completed a three-year residency program in non-domestic animal medicine at the University of California, Davis in conjunction with the California Department of Fish and Wildlife.

Then, in fulfilling a lifelong dream, Barbara spent a year in East Africa. While working with wildlife in their natural environment, she realized there is so much more to the animals than simply their physical bodies. She wanted to know who they are as spiritual beings. What do they think? How do they feel? What do they know?

This led her to pursue a path of intuitive interspecies communication with animals of all kinds. For years she assisted people in understanding their companion animals, but her passion of communing with wild animals never left. That interest, along with her personal journey of spiritual growth, led to in-depth conversations with elephants. They became her teachers. And so, this book was born.

Barbara lives in Ashland, Oregon. She is currently cohosting a podcast called *Animals and Us: Voices of a New Paradigm* with Avantika Mathur. Together they explore animal consciousness and communication, and interview fascinating people who work with animals and the natural world.

She continues to write, speak, and teach courses. You can learn more at her website: barbarashor.com

Or you can visit the podcast website: animalsandus.com. The podcast is available on most podcast venues.